BRAIN
TEASERS
FOR
BRIGHT
SPARKS

Puzzles and solutions by
Dr Gareth Moore
B.Sc (Hons) M.Phil Ph.D

Illustrations by Jess Bradley
and Adam Linley

Designed and edited by Tall Tree

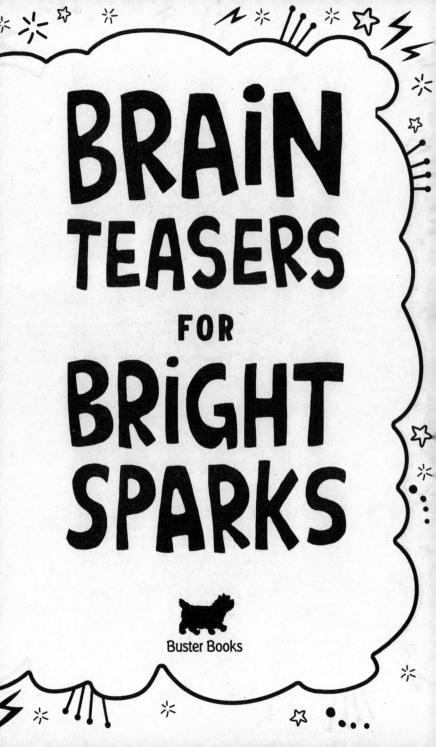

BRAIN TEASERS
FOR
BRIGHT SPARKS

Buster Books

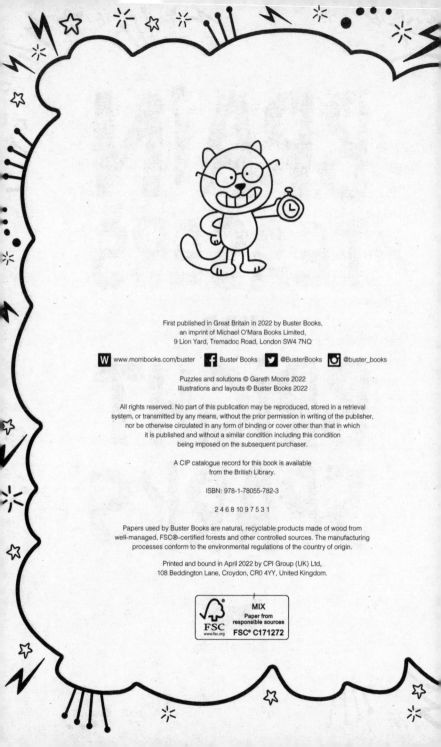

First published in Great Britain in 2022 by Buster Books,
an imprint of Michael O'Mara Books Limited,
9 Lion Yard, Tremadoc Road, London SW4 7NQ

W www.mombooks.com/buster   f Buster Books   🐦 @BusterBooks   📷 @buster_books

Puzzles and solutions © Gareth Moore 2022
Illustrations and layouts © Buster Books 2022

A CIP catalogue record for this book is available
from the British Library.

ISBN: 978-1-78055-782-3

2 4 6 8 10 9 7 5 3 1

Papers used by Buster Books are natural, recyclable products made of wood from
well-managed, FSC®-certified forests and other controlled sources. The manufacturing
processes conform to the environmental regulations of the country of origin.

Printed and bound in April 2022 by CPI Group (UK) Ltd,
108 Beddington Lane, Croydon, CR0 4YY, United Kingdom.

MIX
Paper from
responsible sources
FSC® C171272
FSC
www.fsc.org

INTRODUCTION

This book is packed with more than 80 amazing brain games to challenge you. Are you ready to tackle them?

The puzzles get harder as the book progresses, so it's best to start at the beginning and work your way through. You'll see a little clock symbol at the bottom of each puzzle. Use this space to record how long each game takes you to complete.

The instructions for each brain game will tell you how to get started. If you're not sure what to do, read them again in case there is something you've missed. Many of the brain games also include a finished example that will help you along the way.

There's plenty of space on the pages to make notes as you go, but if you need more room to work out your answers, use the blank pages at the back of the book.

Use a pencil to fill in your answers, then you can change them if you need to.

If you are still stuck, you could also try asking a grown-up. If you're *really* stuck, have a peek at the answers in the back of the book, and then try and work out how you could have got to that solution yourself.

Good luck and have fun!

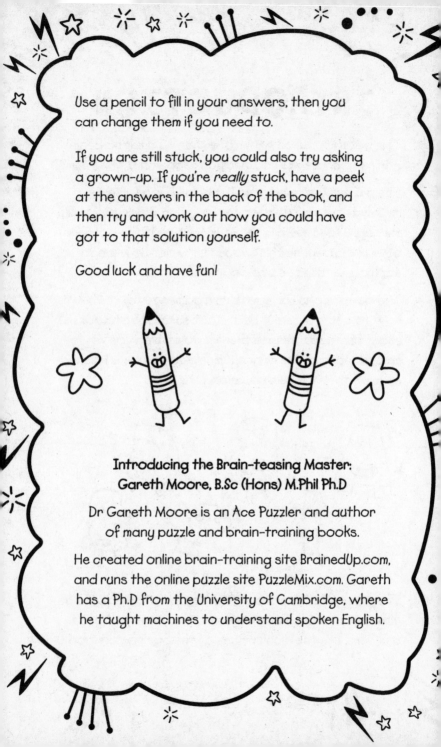

Introducing the Brain-teasing Master: Gareth Moore, B.Sc (Hons) M.Phil Ph.D

Dr Gareth Moore is an Ace Puzzler and author of many puzzle and brain-training books.

He created online brain-training site BrainedUp.com, and runs the online puzzle site PuzzleMix.com. Gareth has a Ph.D from the University of Cambridge, where he taught machines to understand spoken English.

LET THE
BRAIN TEASERS
BEGIN!

SHAPE MATCHING

Below are six shapes, plus the same six shapes cut in half.

Can you draw lines to connect each full shape with its halved version?

One pair has been joined already, to show you how it works.

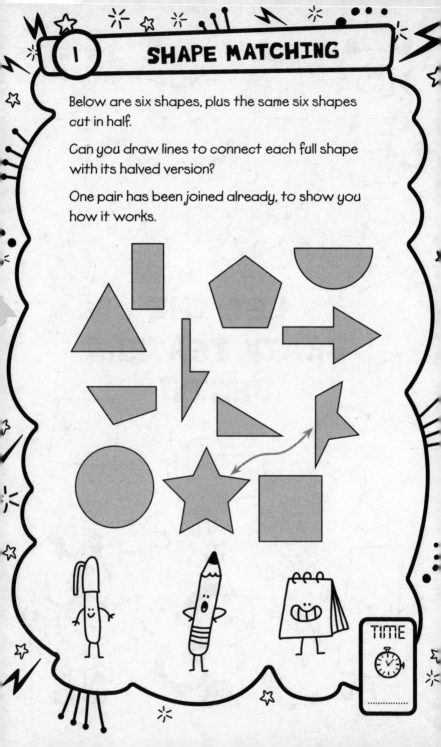

TIME

PYRAMID QUIZ

Fill in the empty squares to complete these number pyramids. Every square must contain a number equal to the sum of the numbers in the two blocks directly beneath it. So, in the example, the 14 at the top is equal to the sum of the 7 and 7 directly beneath it.

EXAMPLE:

	14	
7		7
3	4	3

I.

	8	
2		5

2.

	9	
4		
	2	

3.

13		
	6	
5		

4.

	6		
3	4		5

TIME

....

Complete this loop by placing six of the eight loose dominoes into the shaded spaces. Every domino must be placed so that both ends are next to a different domino with the same number of spots.

Two of the loose dominoes will be left over.

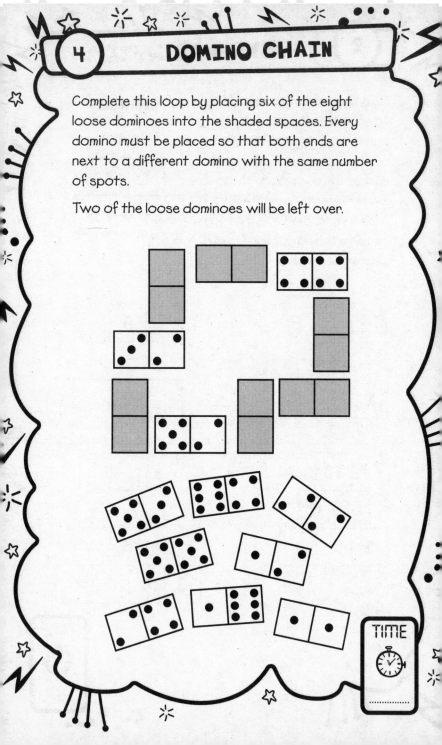

WATER WORLD QUIZ

1. Which of the world's oceans is always partly covered in ice?

a. The Indian Ocean
b. The Pacific Ocean
c. The Arctic Ocean
d. The Atlantic Ocean

2. 'Hammerhead', 'Great White', 'Tiger' and 'Whale' are all kinds of what underwater creature?

a. Dolphin
b. Jellyfish
c. Squid
d. Shark

3. What is the name of the world's largest living structure, found underwater off the east coast of Australia?

a. The Great Barrier Reef
b. The Giant Coral Nest
c. The Pacific Ridge
d. The Watery Mountain

4. How much of the surface of the Earth is covered by water?

a. Less than one quarter
b. Around one third
c. Around half
d. More than two thirds

5. Which of the following is responsible for the tides that make the sea flow in and out each day?

a. Mars
b. The Moon
c. Aliens
d. People jumping

TIME

....

NUMBER PUZZLE

Each of these puzzles contains some numbers and some empty squares. Can you write 1, 2, 3 or 4 into each empty square so that no number repeats in any row or column? Numbers also can't repeat in any of the 2x2 boxes, marked by bold lines.

Notice how in the example solution none of the numbers repeat in any of the marked areas.

Column

2x2 box

EXAMPLE:

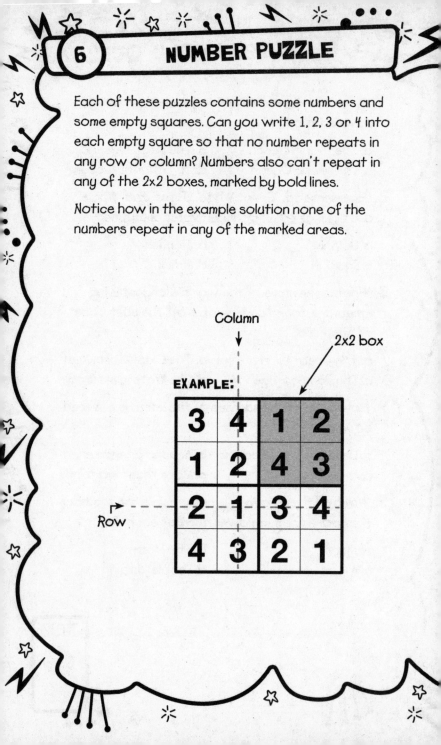

Row

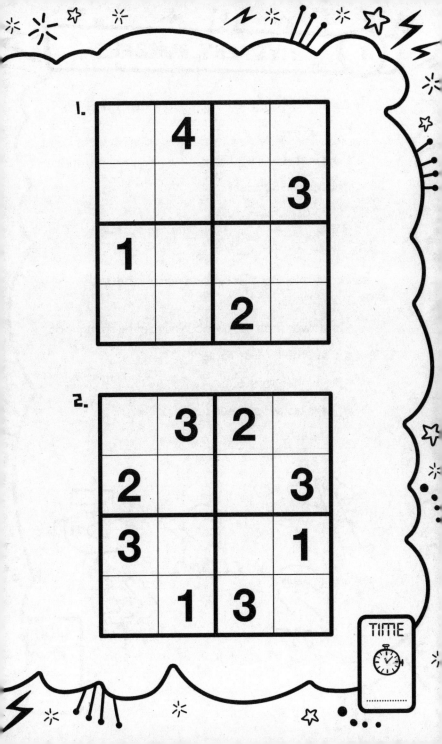

1. Zac is thinking of a number between 1 and 15.

- It's an even number.
- It's in the 5 times table.

What is the number?

....

2. Zac is thinking of a second number between 1 and 15.

- It's lower than the previous number he thought of.
- It's in the 4 times table.
- It's higher than 5.

What is his second number?

....

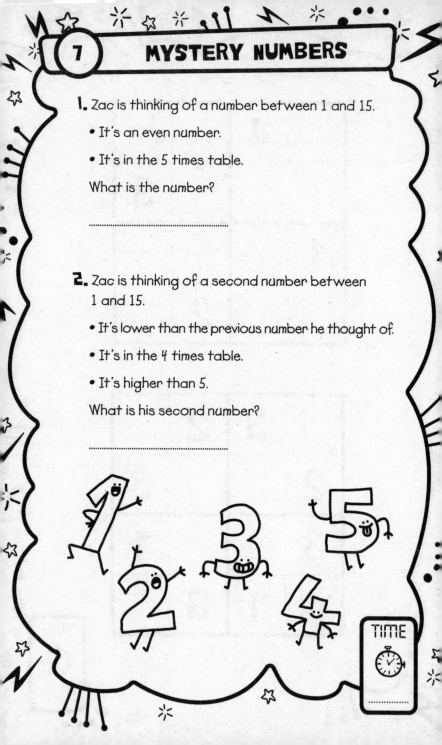

TIME

....

MISSING PIECES

This jigsaw isn't quite finished, but the remaining pieces have been muddled up with those from a different puzzle. Can you work out which are the correct three pieces to complete the picture?

A.

B.

C.

D.

E.

F.

TIME

9   NUMBER SEARCH

Can you find all of the listed numbers in the grid? They can be written in any direction, including diagonally, and can read either forwards or backwards.

33845	54590	67579	70166	71334
47259	66944	68078	71025	76409

3	8	6	7	3	5	3	5
6	1	5	6	4	5	7	9
7	7	4	5	9	0	9	5
5	1	9	8	1	4	4	2
7	0	3	6	7	8	4	7
9	2	6	3	3	0	6	4
8	5	4	3	4	3	8	6
7	7	6	4	0	9	8	6

TIME

....

LAST NUMBER STANDING

Can you eliminate all of the numbers in this grid until only one remains?

- Shade in all the numbers in the 5 times table

- Next, shade in all the remaining numbers which are less than 10

- Finally, shade in all the remaining even numbers

Which is the only number left?

....

2	10	14	8
1	13	3	5
12	6	15	16
20	4	9	7

TIME

....

PAIRING UP

Can you join these objects into pairs by drawing straight lines? The lines can't be diagonal, and they can't cross over other lines or other objects.

Each line must link two different objects.

Here's an example to show how it works:

EXAMPLE:

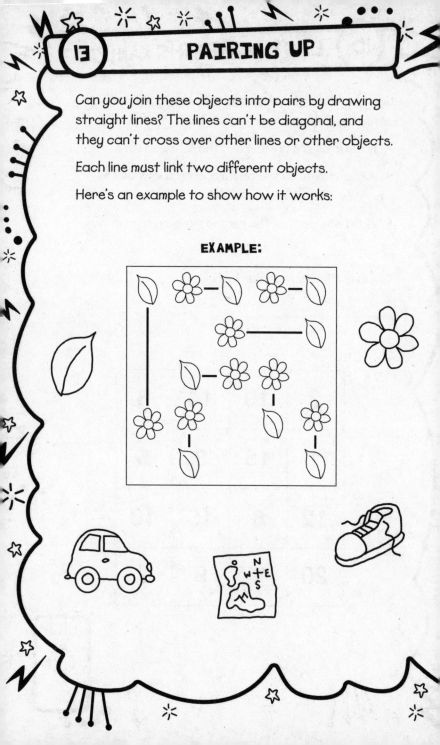

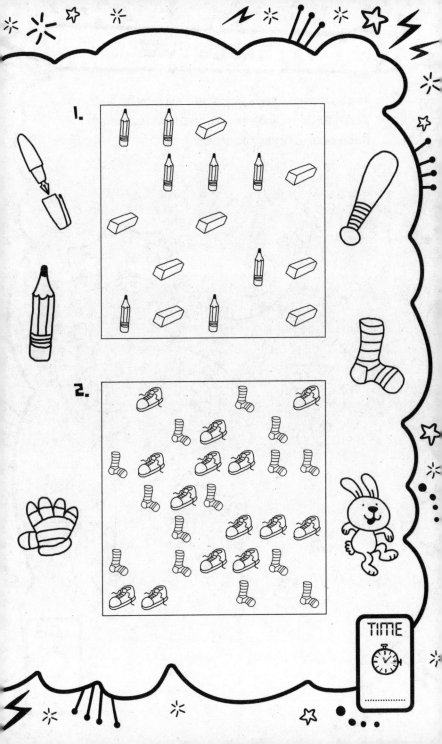

BADGE PUZZLE

14

These badges have each been broken in half. Can you draw lines to join the two halves of each badge back together?

TIME

NUMBER FIT

Fit all of the listed numbers into the grid, writing one digit per square so that every number can be read either across or down the grid. Cross off each number as you place it.

One is placed already to get you going.

4 Digits:	5 Digits:	7 Digits:
4073	66818	4086978
5880		4708378
7079		~~7908640~~
7848		

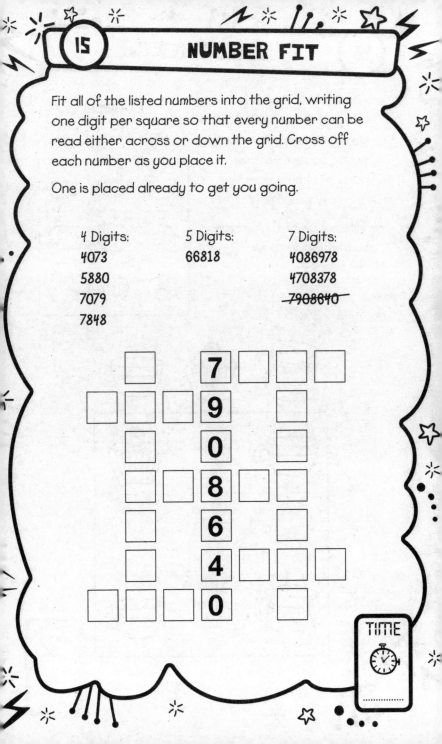

For each of these puzzles, can you place one of the given objects into each empty square so that none of them repeat in any row or column?

Take a look at the example solution to see how this works.

EXAMPLE:

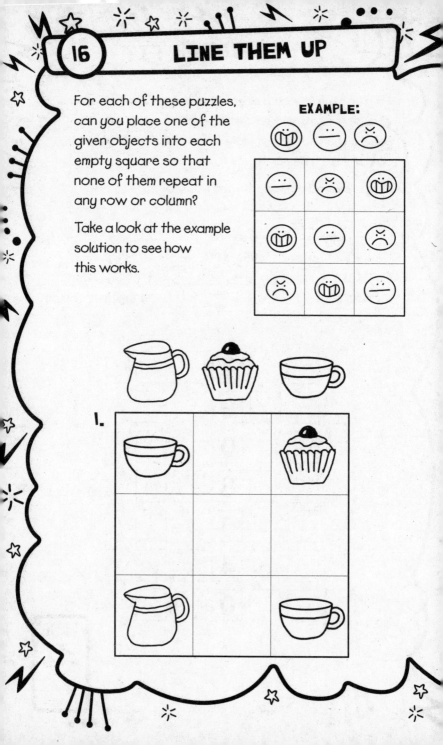

1.

2.

ALIEN QUEUE

Three aliens – Zib, Zab and Zob – are queueing to board a spaceship to planet Zepple.

Each of the aliens has a different-coloured light on its head. One has a blue light, one has a green light and one has a red light.

You notice that:

• Zob is at the back of the queue, and has a blue light

• The alien at the front of the queue has a red light

• Zib is in the middle of the queue

Using the information above, answer these questions:

• Which alien is at the front of the queue?

....

• What colour light does Zib have on its head?

....

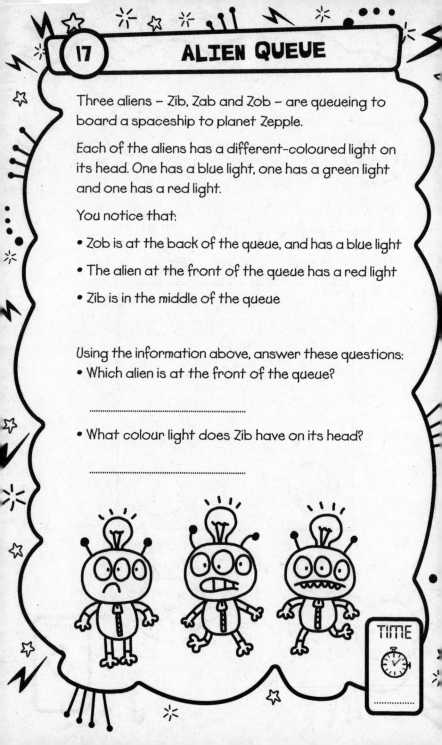

TIME

The picture below is made up of six overlapping circles, but only two of them are of exactly the same size.

Which two?

MYSTERY MAZE

How quickly can you find your way through this maze, entering at the top and exiting at the bottom?

Start

Finish

TIME

These little animals want to fly, but to get off the ground they must buy balloons from the balloon seller.

For each animal, which numbered balloons should they choose so that they add up to the exact total required for that animal? The balloon seller won't sell any number more than once to the same animal. The balloon seller has the following balloons available:

Write your answers on to the balloons.

The balloon seller has these balloons: 4, 5, 8, 10, 12

1. = 9

2. = 20

3. = 21

4. = 29

TIME

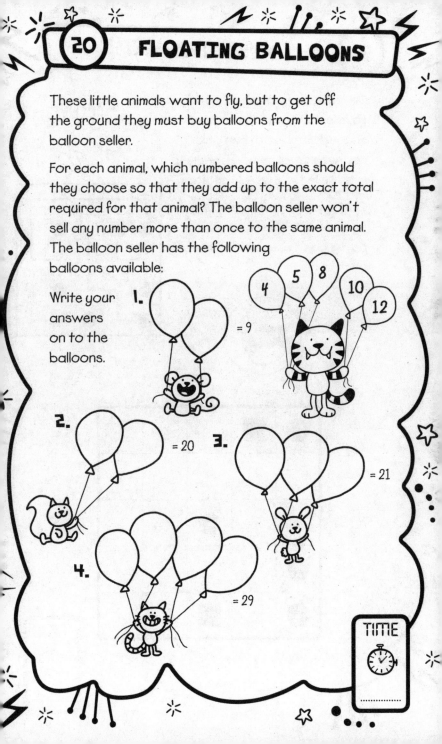

FIND THE PATH

Can you draw a set of paths to join each pair of identical shapes? Each path can only use horizontal or vertical lines, just like in the example solution.

Only one path can enter any square, which means that paths can't cross or touch each other.

EXAMPLE:
Notice how this path links the pair of circles

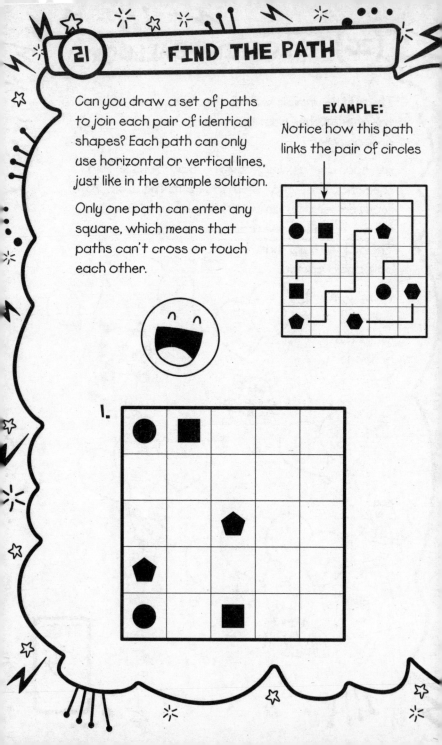

I.

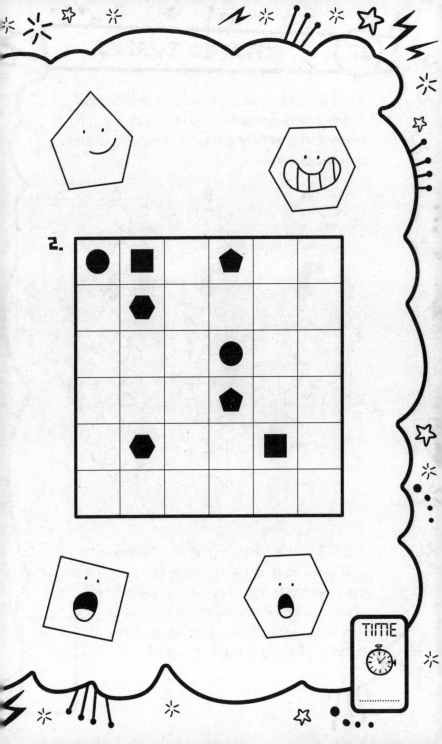

What would pictures A, B and C each look like if rotated 90 degrees clockwise as shown by the arrow? Which of the options, 1 to 3, shows each rotated picture?

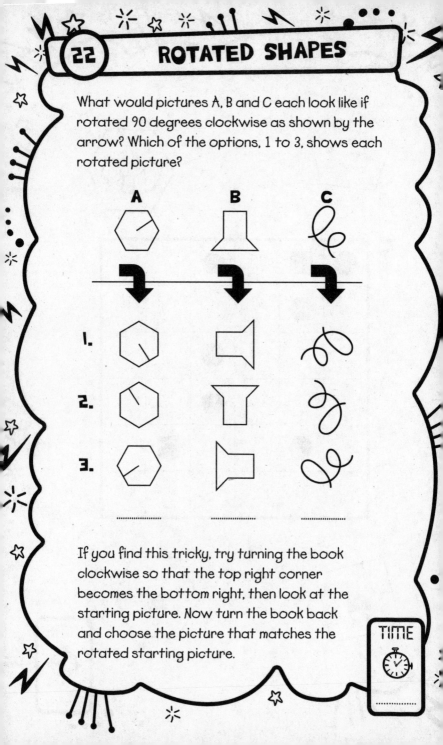

A   **B**   **C**

1.

2.

3.

....

If you find this tricky, try turning the book clockwise so that the top right corner becomes the bottom right, then look at the starting picture. Now turn the book back and choose the picture that matches the rotated starting picture.

TIME

Can you spot all five differences between these two pictures?

TIME

FENCE PROBLEM

Can you complete both of these loop puzzles, so that every dot is visited exactly once?

Each loop can only use horizontal or vertical lines and cannot cross over or touch itself.

EXAMPLE:

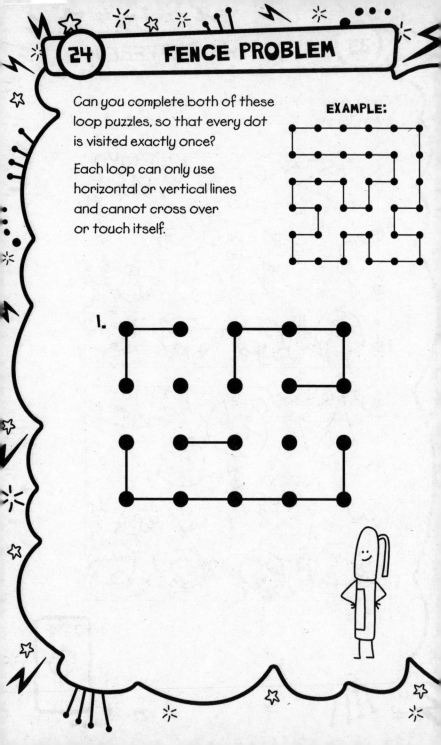

1.

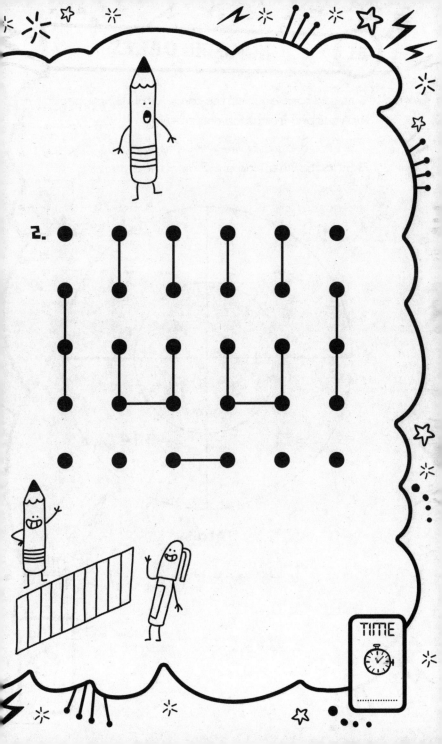

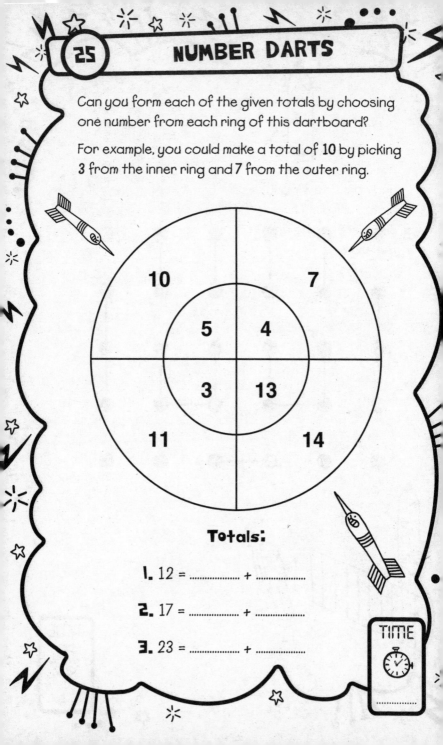

NUMBER DARTS

Can you form each of the given totals by choosing one number from each ring of this dartboard?

For example, you could make a total of **10** by picking **3** from the inner ring and **7** from the outer ring.

Dartboard:

Outer ring: 10, 7, 11, 14
Inner ring: 5, 4, 3, 13

Totals:

1. 12 = ... + ...

2. 17 = ... + ...

3. 23 = ... + ...

TIME

....

COUNTING CUBES

You have 8 blocks built into a 2x2x2 tower.

Then you take away the 3 paler blocks, and count how many blocks remain. There are 5 left, as shown in the example.

EXAMPLE:

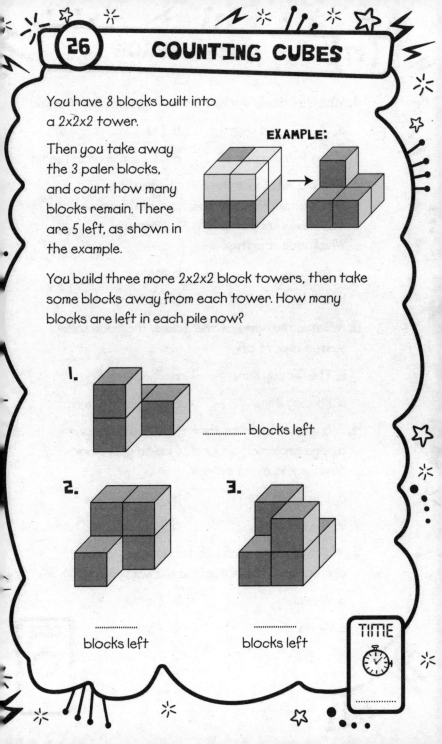

You build three more 2x2x2 block towers, then take some blocks away from each tower. How many blocks are left in each pile now?

1.

.... blocks left

2.

....
blocks left

3.

....
blocks left

TIME

....

1. Which of these options correctly describes the Sun?

    a. The Sun is a star   b. The Sun is a comet

    c. The Sun is a planet   d. The Sun is an asteroid

2. In 2020, NASA launched a robot called *Perseverance* into space, to explore a planet sometimes known as 'the Red Planet'. Which planet is this?

    a. Neptune   b. Mars

    c. Saturn   d. Mercury

3. What is the name of the galaxy that our solar system is part of?

    a. The Cloudy Burst   b. The Milky Way

    c. The Icy Zone   d. The Dusty Swirl

4. Many astronomers think the universe began with a huge explosion around 14 billion years ago. What is this event called?

    a. The Giant Pop   b. The Huge Boom

    c. The Big Bang   d. The Massive Thud

5. Which planet, which orbits between Mercury and Earth, is the hottest in the solar system?

    a. Neptune   b. Jupiter

    c. Venus   d. Mars

TIME

Imagine merging these two pictures, so that the empty squares in picture A were replaced with the filled squares in picture B.

How many stars would you be able to count in the merged picture?

....

A   B

TIME

MIRROR IMAGE

Imagine the horizontal line under each of these shapes, A to C, is a mirror. Which of the options, 1, 2 or 3, would be the result of reflecting each shape in that mirror?

You can hold the book up to a real mirror to help you if you get stuck.

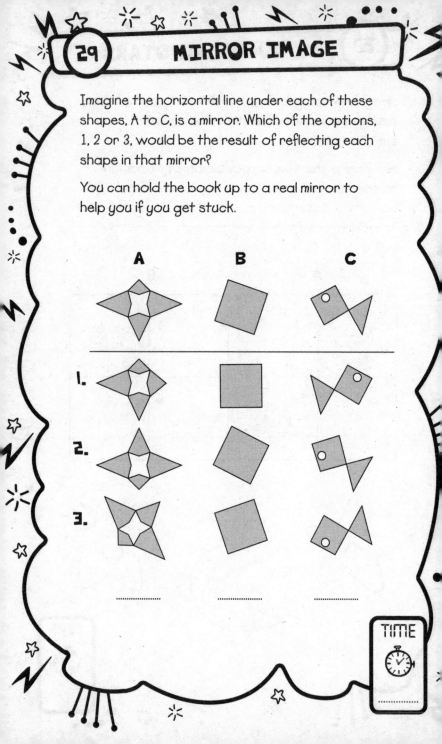

A **B** **C**

I.

2.

3.

....

TIME

....

BRAIN CHAINS

Here are some fun mental arithmetic puzzles to test your number skills.

Begin with the number at the top of each puzzle and apply all of the instructions in turn, from top to bottom. Keep going until you reach the empty box at the bottom, then write your answer there. To make it extra tricky, try to do all of the sums in your head without writing anything down until each final answer.

In the first puzzle, for example, start with **19**, then add **14** (to make **33**), then subtract **12** (to make **21**) and so on.

19	**13**	**5**
+14	+10	×6
-12	×2	÷5
÷3	-7	÷2
-4	×2	×7
×2	-12	$×\frac{1}{3}$

TIME

....

FULL OR EMPTY

You have a row of seven cups in front of you.

The first four cups in the row have water in them, while the three cups on the right are empty.

If you are only allowed to touch two cups – and nothing else at all – then how can you change the cups so that they alternate between full and empty?

When you are done the cups should be full, empty, full, empty, full, empty and then full, when looked at in order.

....

....

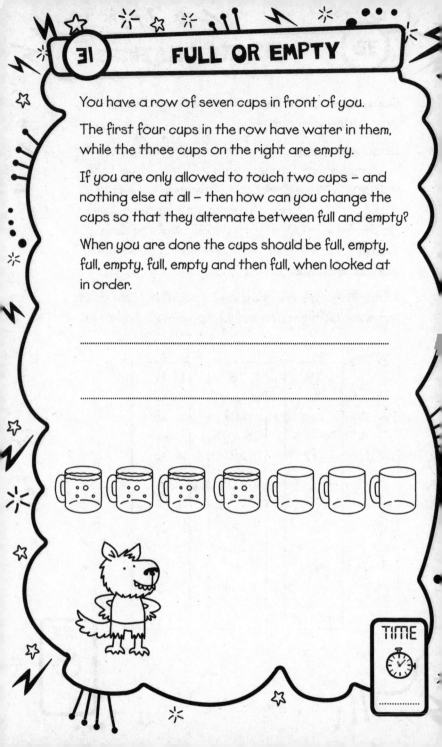

TIME

Can you find all of the listed numbers in the grid?

They can be written in any direction, including diagonally, and can read either forwards or backwards.

13807	41314	70436	77020
18198	49000	73859	90981
29813	5814	76854	93189

6	4	7	3	1	8	3	0	7	3
6	1	8	8	1	1	9	1	4	9
9	7	9	4	8	8	9	9	4	3
0	0	4	9	9	0	1	5	4	1
9	2	2	1	9	0	8	1	4	8
7	7	0	5	3	6	0	1	8	9
5	4	8	7	7	1	8	0	9	4
6	3	4	0	7	5	4	9	1	8
7	1	3	8	0	7	0	4	8	3
0	1	9	6	7	8	1	2	1	1

TIME

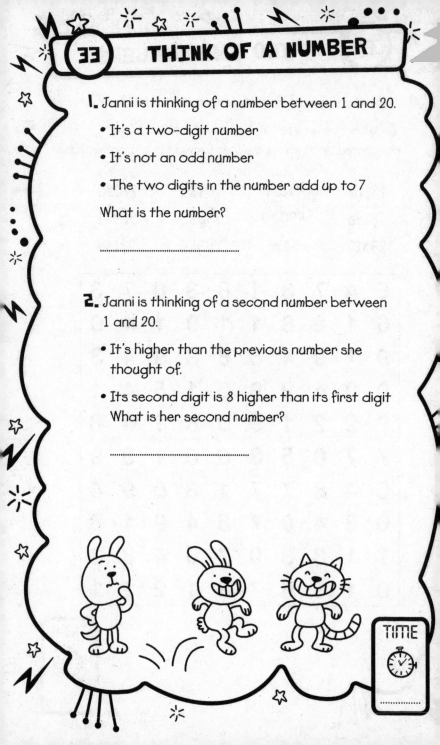

THINK OF A NUMBER

1. Janni is thinking of a number between 1 and 20.

- It's a two-digit number
- It's not an odd number
- The two digits in the number add up to 7

What is the number?

....

2. Janni is thinking of a second number between 1 and 20.

- It's higher than the previous number she thought of.
- Its second digit is 8 higher than its first digit

What is her second number?

....

TIME

MAZE PUZZLE

How quickly can you travel through this maze, entering at the top and exiting at the bottom?

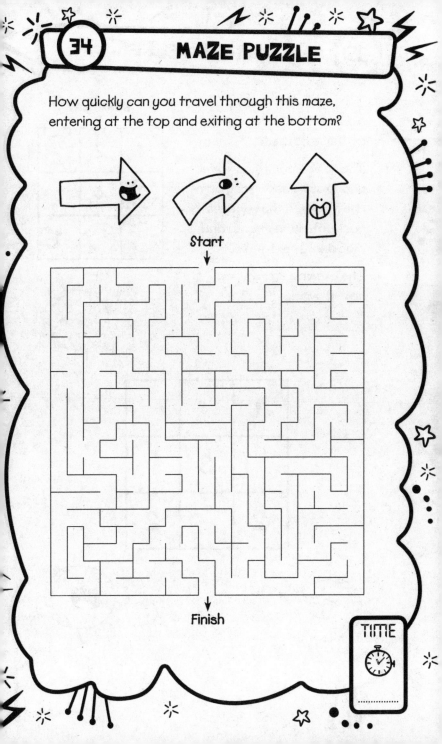

Start

Finish

TIME

Can you find the coins hidden in the empty squares of these puzzles?

The numbers in the grid tell you exactly how many coins are hidden in the squares horizontally, vertically and diagonally next to it.

The example shows you how it works.

EXAMPLE:

1	2	◯
◯	4	
◯	◯	1

I.

1		
	3	
2		2

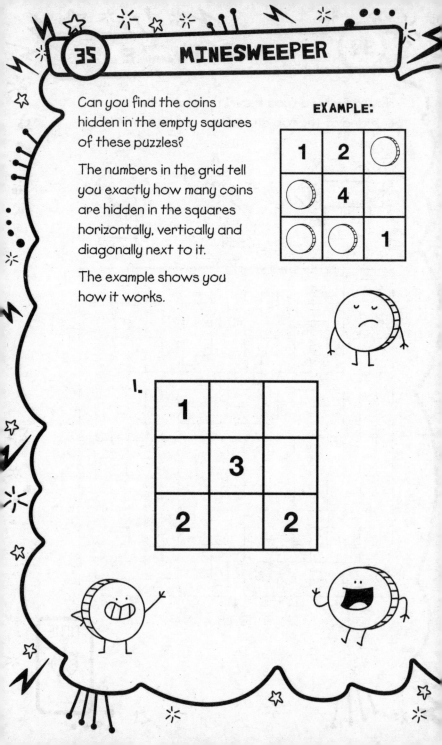

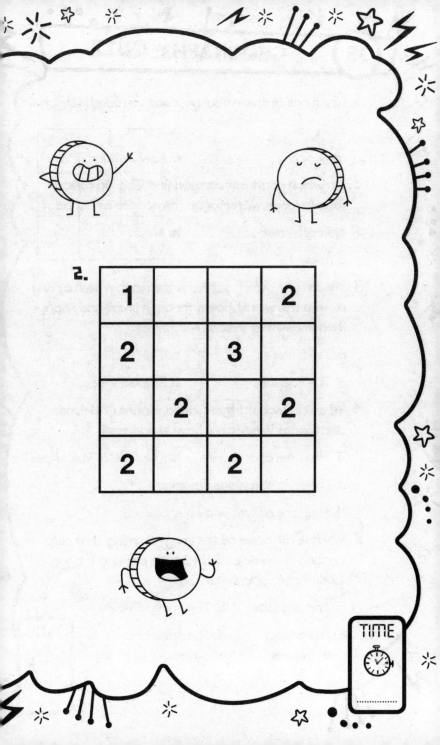

GEOGRAPHY QUIZ

1. Which one of these countries can be found in Europe?

    a. Japan   b. France

    c. Mexico   d. New Zealand

2. On which continent can you find Niagara Falls, a famous large waterfall on the border of Canada?

    a. North America   b. Africa

    c. Asia   d. Europe

3. Which river, which contains the most water of any river in the world, flows through Brazil and shares its name with a famous rainforest?

    a. The Thames   b. The Danube

    c. The Amazon   d. The Ganges

4. What do Mount Etna, Kilauea, Mount St Helens and Mount Vesuvius all have in common?

    a. They are all countries   b. They are all volcanoes

    c. They are all famous buildings

    d. They are all well-known explorers

5. What is the name of the imaginary ring that runs around the middle of the Earth, passing through 13 different countries?

    a. The equator   b. The Arctic Circle

    c. The tropic   d. The Antarctic
       of Cancer   Circle

TIME

PLACE THE NUMBERS

Fit all of the listed numbers into the grid, writing one digit per square so that every number can be read either across or down the grid.

Cross off each number as you place it.

One is placed already to get you going.

3 Digits:	5 Digits:	6 Digits:	7 Digits:
238	28307	452742	2630888
356	44239	616452	9372051
	81102		
	85044		

8 1 1 0 2

TIME

How good are you at drawing loops? In each puzzle, draw a single loop that visits every white square but none of the black squares. The loop cannot enter any square more than once, and can't travel diagonally.

EXAMPLE:

I.

HALF SHAPES

Below are six shapes, plus the same six shapes cut in half.

Can you draw lines to connect each full shape with its halved version? Some of the halved shapes have been rotated.

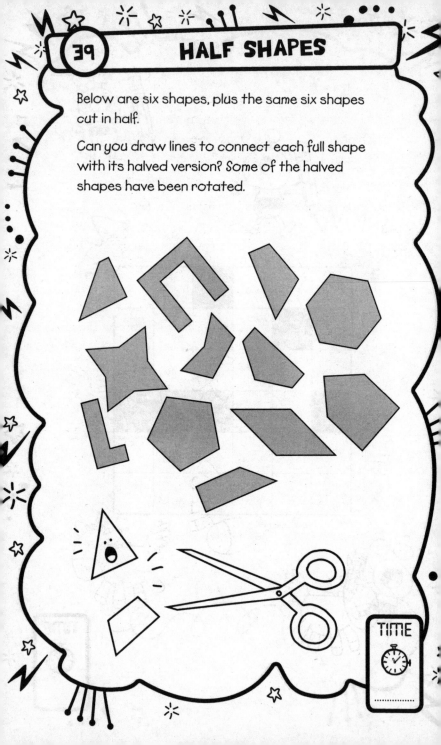

TIME

UNICORN PAIRS

A set of toy unicorns has become mixed up. You know that there are two of each type of unicorn, so can you draw lines to join the unicorns into identical pairs?

You'll need to look out for small differences between each design of unicorn.

TIME

NUMBER PATH

For each puzzle, place a number into each empty square so that every number from 1 to 16 is used once. The numbers must be placed so that they form a path from 1 to 16, moving in any direction from square to square except diagonally.

EXAMPLE:

5	4	3	2
6	7	8	1
15	14	9	10
16	13	12	11

Take a look at the example to see how this works.

You can cross off the numbers you've already used on the list underneath each puzzle, if you like.

I.

	16		10
	13		9
3		1	
4		6	

X 2 X X 5 X 7 8 X X
11 12 X 14 15 X

2.

4			7
	14		
		16	
1			10

~~1~~ 2 3 ~~4~~ 5 6 ~~7~~ 8 9 ~~10~~
11 12 13 ~~14~~ 15 ~~16~~

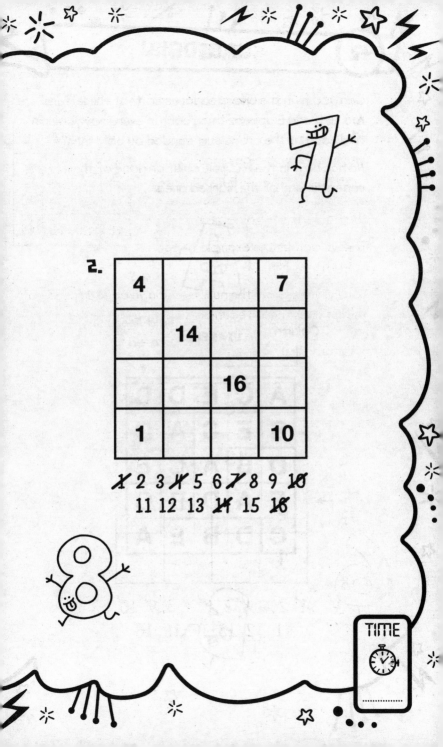

JIGDOKU

Can you fill in the empty squares so that the letters A, B, C, D and E appear once each in every row, column and each of the areas surrounded by bold lines?

Notice how in the example solution none of the letters repeat in any of the marked areas.

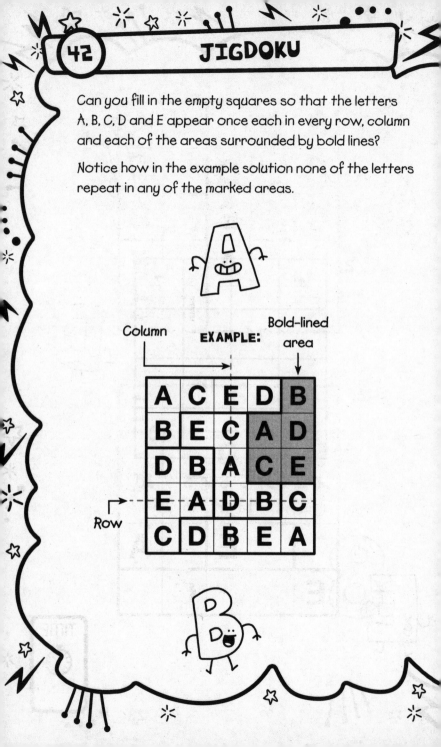

Column

EXAMPLE:

Bold-lined area

A	C	E	D	B
B	E	C	A	D
D	B	A	C	E
E	A	D	B	C
C	D	B	E	A

Row

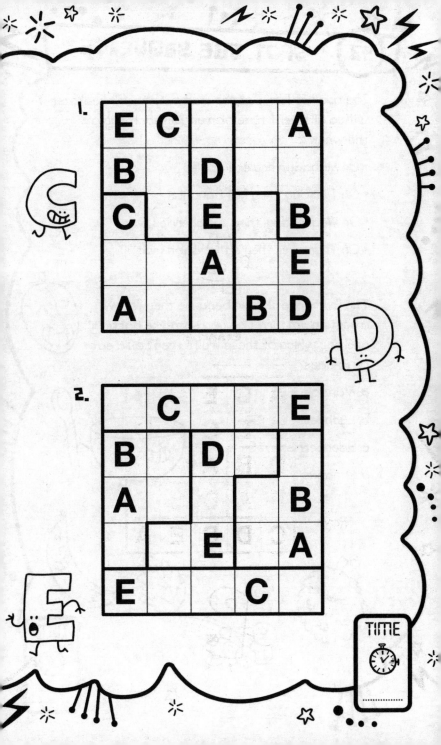

Zoe and her family all eat fruit with their breakfast, with a different type of fruit for each day of the week.

- On Monday, they eat apples
- On Tuesday, they eat bananas
- On Wednesday, they eat cherries
- On Thursday, they eat dragon fruit

The fruits are chosen because they follow a certain pattern. Can you spot the pattern, and say which of these fruits they could eat on Fridays?

a. Mangos

b. Lychees

c. Elderberries

d. Bananas

....

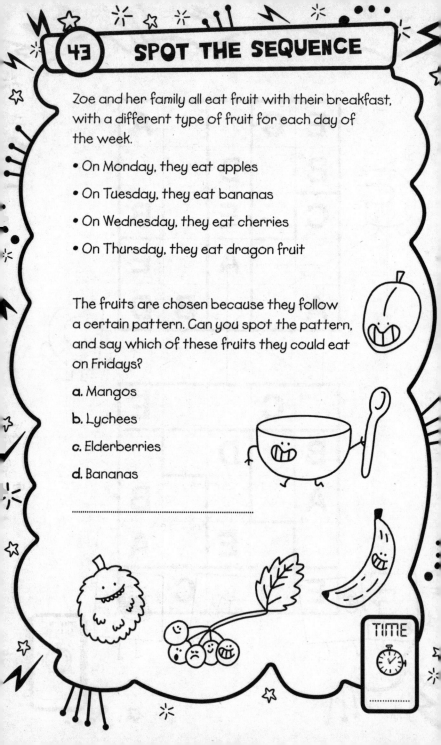

TIME

SHAPE COUNTING

It's time to test your shape-counting skills again.

Take a look at this picture. How many triangles of all different sizes can you count in the picture? Some of them overlap each other, so there are more than you might think.

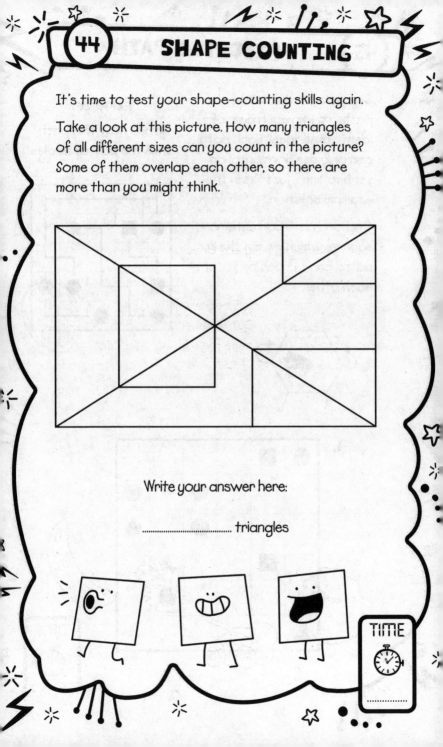

Write your answer here:

.... triangles

TIME

Can you draw a set of paths to join each pair of identical shapes? Each path can only use horizontal or vertical lines, just like in the example solution.

Only one path can enter any square, which means that paths can't cross or touch each other.

EXAMPLE:

Notice how this path links the pair of circles.

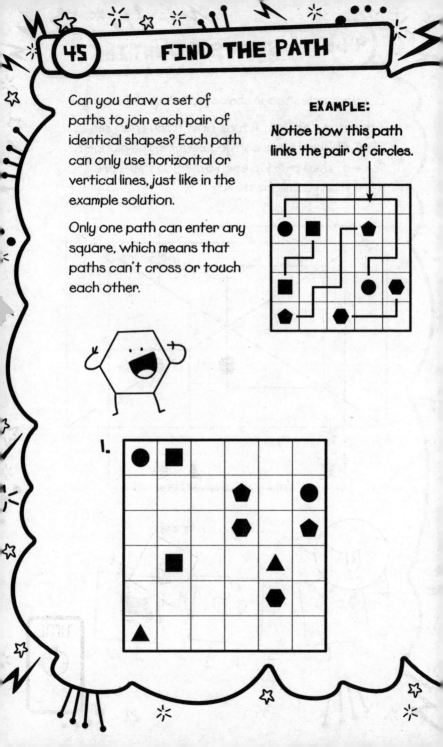

I.

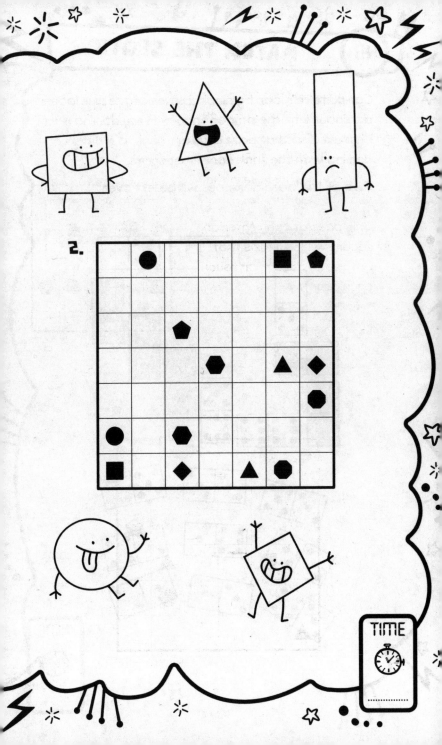

MATCH THE SPOTS

Complete this loop by placing seven of the nine loose dominoes into the shaded spaces. Every domino must be placed so that both ends are next to a different domino with the same number of spots.

Two of the loose dominoes will be left over.

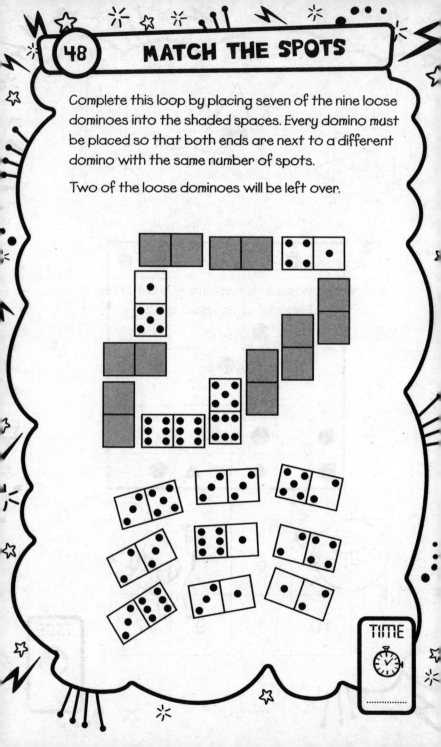

TIME

NUMBER ELIMINATION

Can you eliminate all of the numbers in this grid until only one remains?

- Shade in all the numbers in the **3** times table.

- Next, shade in any number which is in the **5** times table.

- Shade in all the squares in any columns in which the remaining numbers add up to a total of **15** (a column is a vertical row of squares).

- There should be only two numbers left. Shade in the one which is lower in value.

Which is the only number left?

....

5	15	4	8
12	2	3	24
18	6	11	20
10	1	9	7

TIME

....

NUMBER QUIZ

Each of these puzzles contains some numbers and some empty squares. Can you write 1, 2, 3, 4, 5 or 6 into each empty square so that no number repeats in any row or column? Numbers also can't repeat in any of the 3x2 boxes, marked by bold lines.

Notice how in the example solution none of the numbers repeat in any of the marked areas.

EXAMPLE:

Column

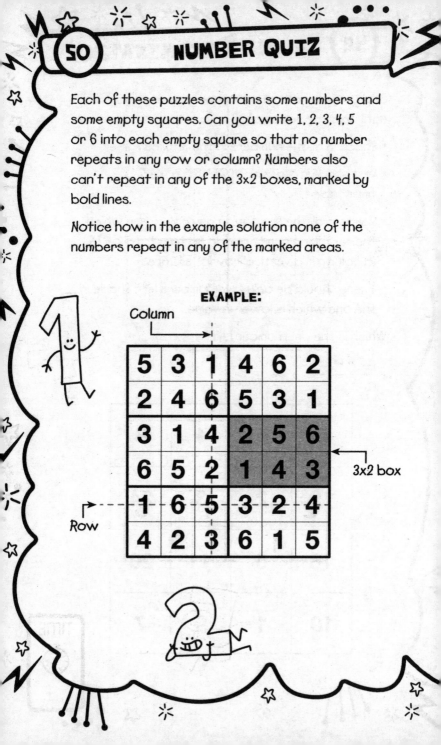

5	3	1	4	6	2
2	4	6	5	3	1
3	1	4	2	5	6
6	5	2	1	4	3
1	6	5	3	2	4
4	2	3	6	1	5

← 3x2 box

Row

1.

		6	4		
	1	4	2	5	
6	3			2	4
5	4			1	3
	2	3	1	6	
		5	3		

2.

	2			3	
1		4	2		6
	5			4	
	6			1	
2		5	1		3
	1			2	

TIME

....

COIN PATTERNS

In front of you are four identical coins:

How would you rearrange these four coins so that all four coins are each touching every other coin?

If you can't work it out in your head, try getting four real coins – or four counters from a game – to see if that helps.

TIME

TRIANGLE QUIZ

The picture below is made up of seven overlapping triangles, but only two of them are of exactly the same size. Which two?

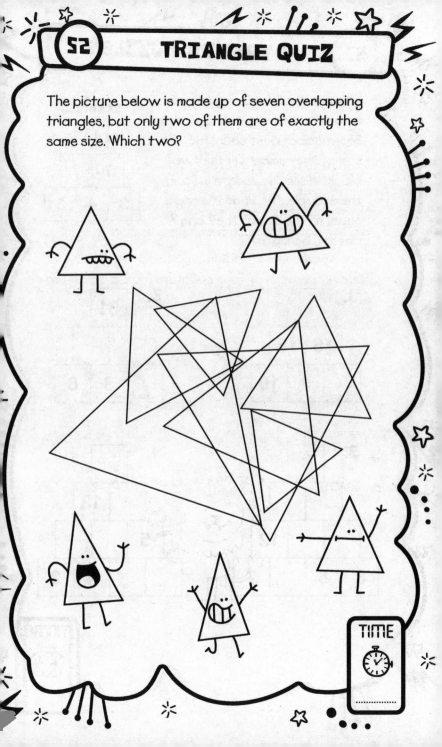

TIME

Fill in the empty squares to complete these number pyramids. Each number must equal the sum of the numbers in the two blocks directly beneath it. So, in the example, the 14 at the top is equal to the sum of the 7 and 7 directly beneath it.

EXAMPLE:

14		
7	7	
3	4	3

I.

16	18	
		10

2.

31	
8	6

3.

	12
8	6		7

4.

	13
5	
	4	2

TIME

....

Fit all of the listed numbers into the grid, writing one digit per square so that every number can be read either across or down the grid.

Cross off each number as you place it. One is placed already to get you going.

3 Digits:		4 Digits:	5 Digits:	7 Digits:
198	613	2385	38094	3306808
2̶5̶1̶	891	3043	58620	8174319
284	906	3422	74677	8991744
423	980	8018	83579	9416623

TIME

....

For each of these puzzles, can you place one of the given objects into each empty square so that none of them repeat in any row or column?

Take a look at the example solution to see how this works.

EXAMPLE:

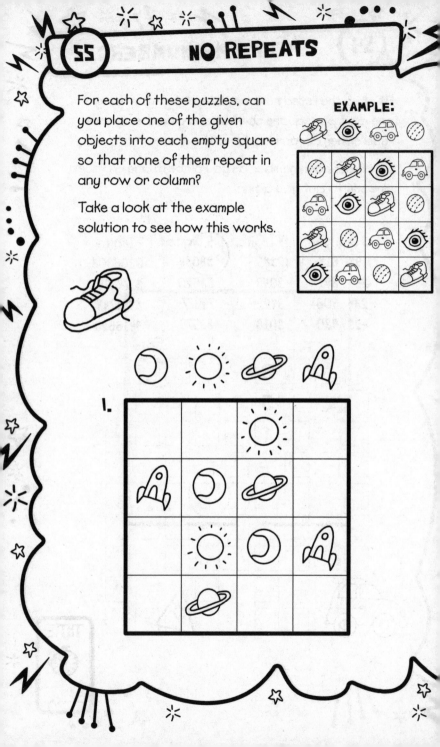

I.

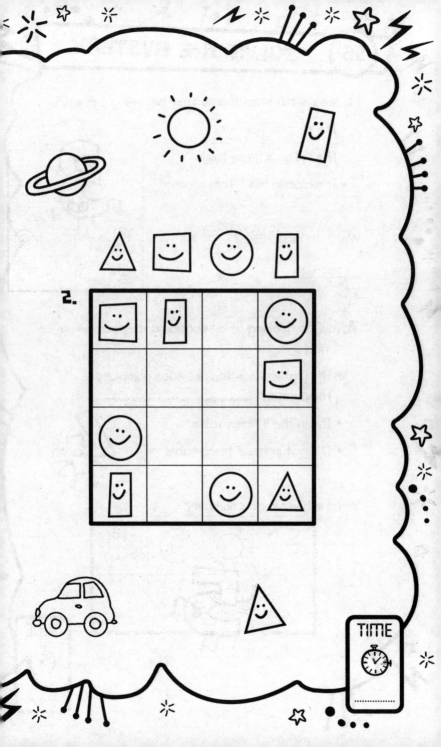

1. Meg is thinking of a number between 1 and 25.

- It's an odd number
- It's in the 3 times table
- It's also in the 5 times table

What is the number?

....

2. Meg is thinking of a second number between 1 and 25.

- It's higher than the previous number she thought of
- It's in the 4 times table
- It's not in the 8 times table

What is her second number?

....

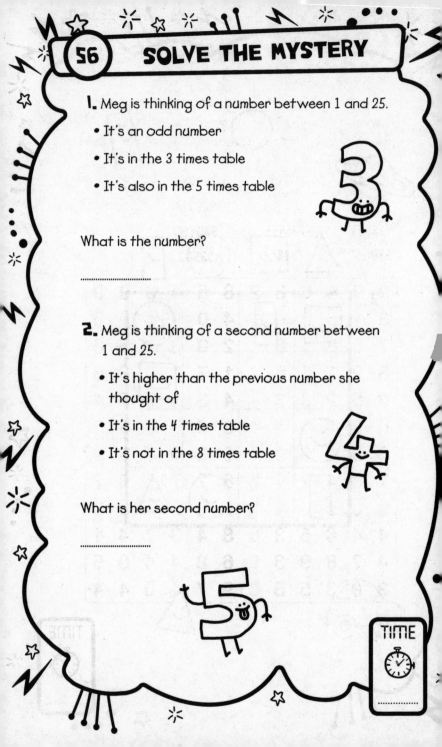

TIME

....

FIND THE NUMBERS

Can you find all of the listed numbers in the grid?
They can be written in any direction, including
diagonally, and can read either forwards or backwards.

260615	651189	780287	974044
446581	661246	926937	994682
453559	735445	930490	
536627	738872	93580	

9	9	4	6	8	2	8	5	4	3	9	9
5	1	6	0	6	2	4	0	9	4	5	0
7	5	8	1	8	4	2	8	0	7	5	6
8	9	7	5	5	3	1	7	3	3	3	8
2	5	2	3	3	1	4	3	8	5	5	4
0	6	7	6	5	6	6	4	9	8	4	5
8	9	4	6	9	0	6	6	6	6	3	9
7	3	4	2	1	3	8	2	7	5	9	7
9	6	9	0	1	5	7	6	7	2	8	6
4	4	6	5	3	6	8	4	3	7	4	1
4	7	8	9	3	9	6	8	4	4	0	5
9	9	3	5	8	0	9	7	4	0	4	4

TIME

Can you join these objects into pairs by drawing straight lines? The lines can't be diagonal, and they can't cross over other lines or other objects. Each line must link two different objects.

Here's an example to show how it works:

EXAMPLE:

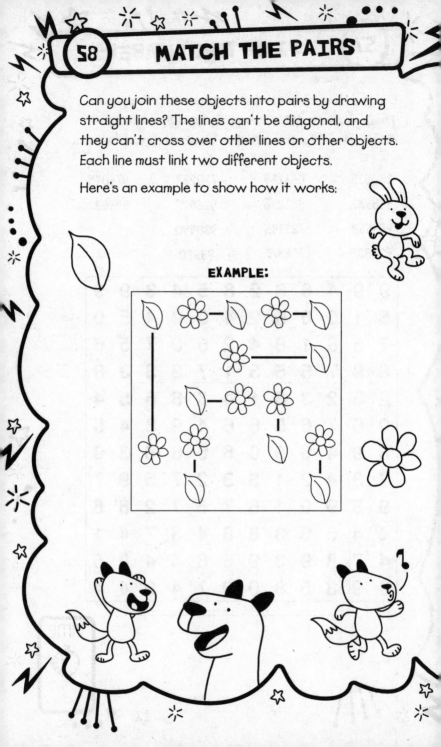

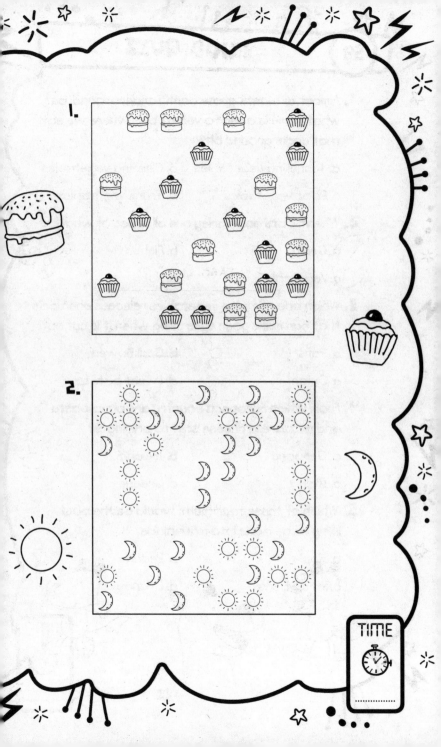

FOOD QUIZ

1. Almost all plants grow partly underground, but what name is given to vegetables where we eat that underground bit?

a. Tunnelling vegetables   b. Climbing vegetables

c. Root vegetables   d. Trunk vegetables

2. Wheat, oats and barley are all types of what?

a. Grain   b. Fish

c. Vegetable   d. Nut

3. Which one of these vegetables releases chemicals that can make your eyes sting when it is cut up?

a. Parsnip   b. Cauliflower

c. Onion   d. Sweet potato

4. From which European country are pizza, pasta and mozzarella cheese said to originate?

a. Germany   b. Ireland

c. Italy   d. Greece

5. Which of these four fruits would be the most likely to be made into marmalade?

a. Apple   b. Peach

c. Strawberry   d. Orange

TIME

Which of these silhouettes exactly matches the picture at the top of the page, apart from in terms of its size?

a.

b.

c.

d.

e.

f.

TIME

NO LINES OF FOUR

Place either an 'X' or an 'O' into each empty square so that there are never more than three 'X's or 'O's in a line in any direction – including diagonally.

EXAMPLE:

O	X	X	O	X
O	O	O	X	X
O	X	O	X	O
X	X	O	X	X
X	X	O	X	X

I.

O	X	O	O	
X	X		O	O
		O	X	O
X	O	X	O	X
	X		X	X

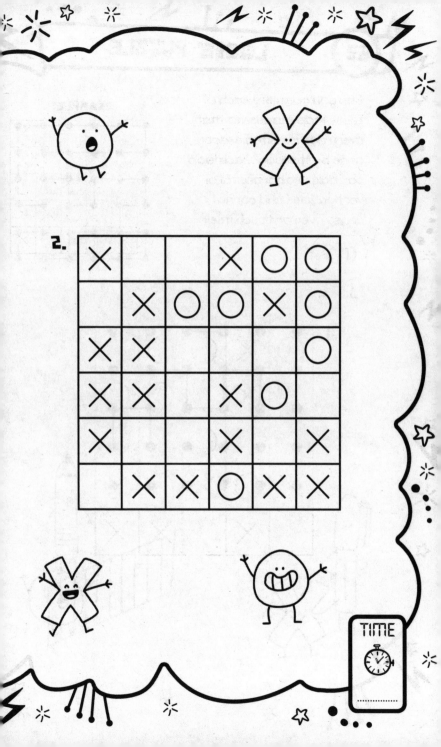

LOOPY PUZZLE

Can you complete each of these loop puzzles, so that every dot is visited exactly once by the loop? Each loop can only use horizontal or vertical lines and cannot cross over or touch itself.

EXAMPLE:

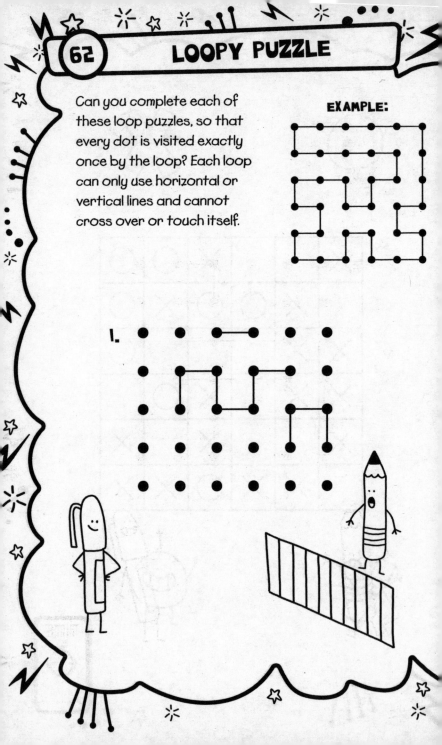

I.

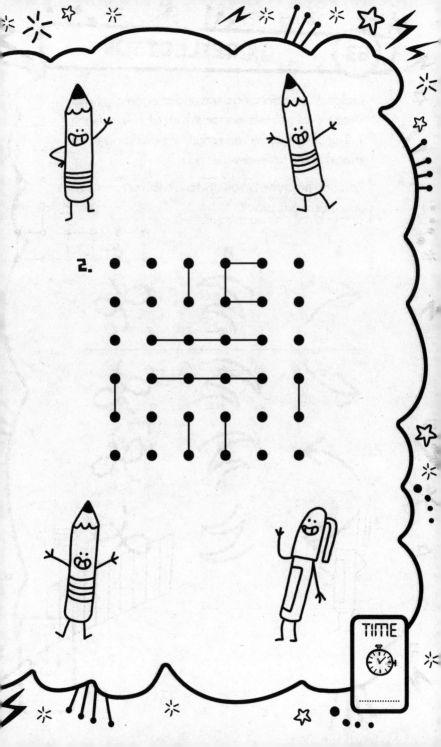

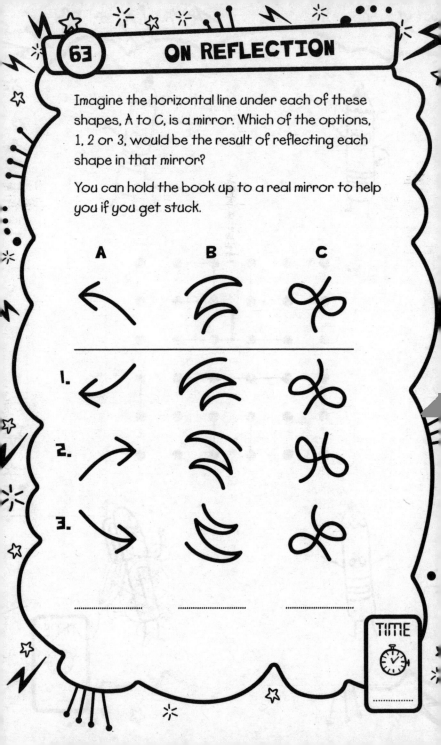

63 ON REFLECTION

Imagine the horizontal line under each of these shapes, A to C, is a mirror. Which of the options, 1, 2 or 3, would be the result of reflecting each shape in that mirror?

You can hold the book up to a real mirror to help you if you get stuck.

A   B   C

1.

2.

3.

TIME

HIT THE MARK

Can you form each of the given totals by choosing one number from each ring of this dartboard?

For example, you could make a total of **20** by picking **7** from the inner ring and **13** from the outer ring.

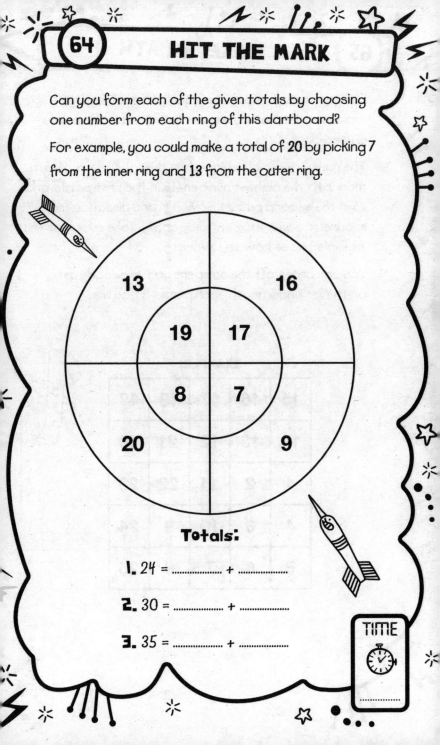

Totals:

1. 24 = ... + ...

2. 30 = ... + ...

3. 35 = ... + ...

TIME

MAKE A PATH

For each puzzle, place a number into each empty square so that every number listed under the puzzle is used once.

The numbers must be placed so that they form a path from 1 to the highest number (16 in the first puzzle, and 25 in the second puzzle), moving in any direction from square to square except diagonally. Take a look at the example to see how this works.

You can cross off the numbers you've already used on the list underneath each puzzle, if you like.

EXAMPLE:

15	16	17	18	19
14	13	12	21	20
1	2	11	22	23
4	3	10	9	24
5	6	7	8	25

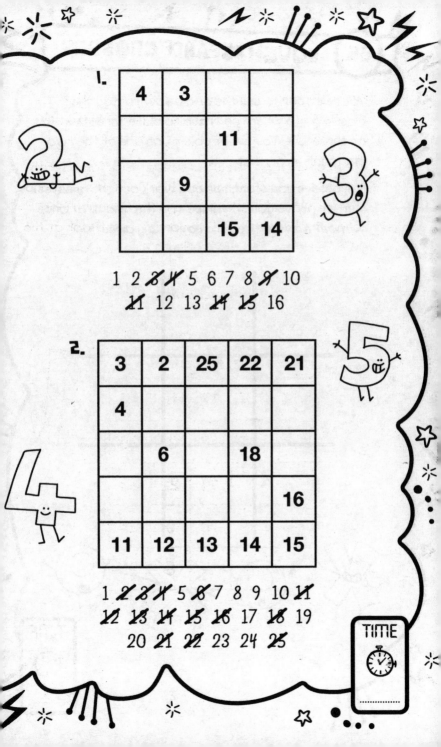

1.

4	3		
		11	
	9		
		15	14

1 2 ~~3~~ ~~4~~ 5 6 7 8 ~~9~~ 10
~~11~~ 12 13 ~~14~~ ~~15~~ 16

2.

3	2	25	22	21
4				
	6		18	
				16
11	12	13	14	15

1 ~~2~~ ~~3~~ ~~4~~ 5 ~~6~~ 7 8 9 10 ~~11~~
~~12~~ ~~13~~ ~~14~~ ~~15~~ ~~16~~ 17 ~~18~~ 19
20 ~~21~~ ~~22~~ 23 24 ~~25~~

TIME
....

You're about to use the grid below to play the classic game where you need to place three 'X's or three 'O's in a row or column, or one of the two diagonals, in order to win.

But, before you start, can you work out the greatest number of 'X's you can place into the grid all at once *without* making three in a *row* in any direction?

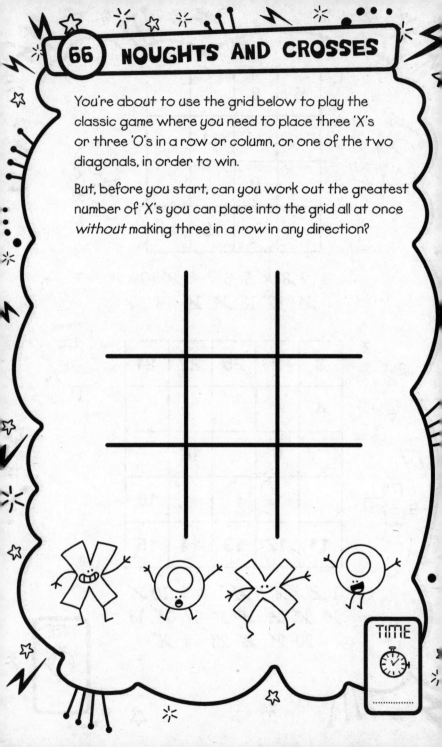

TIME

FLY AWAY

These little animals must buy balloons from the balloon seller so that they can fly.

For each animal, which numbered balloons should they choose so that they add up to the exact total required for that animal? The balloon seller won't sell any number more than once to the same animal. The balloon seller has the following balloons available:

1. = 20

2. = 22

3. = 29

4. = 38

TIME

How good are you at drawing loops? In each puzzle, draw a single loop that visits every white square but none of the black squares. The loop cannot enter any square more than once, and can't travel diagonally.

EXAMPLE:

1.

2.

Amy is at the zoo, and she is visiting the animals in a certain order.

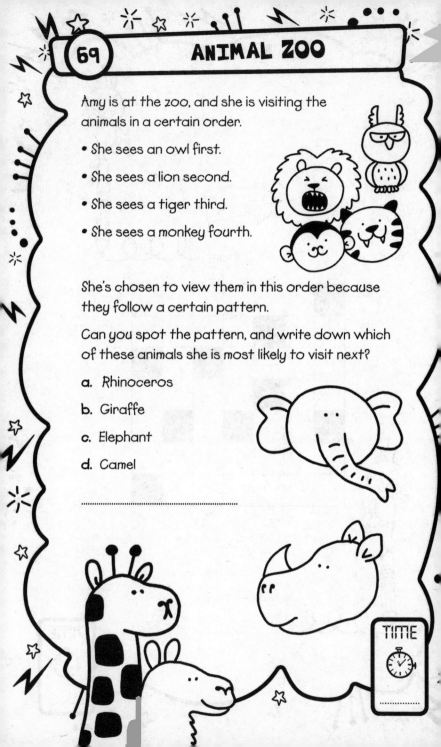

- She sees an owl first.
- She sees a lion second.
- She sees a tiger third.
- She sees a monkey fourth.

She's chosen to view them in this order because they follow a certain pattern.

Can you spot the pattern, and write down which of these animals she is most likely to visit next?

a. Rhinoceros

b. Giraffe

c. Elephant

d. Camel

....

TIME
......

ENTER THE MAZE

How quickly can you find your way through this maze, entering at the top and exiting at the bottom?

Start

Finish

TIME

Here are some fun mental arithmetic puzzles to test your number skills.

Begin with the number at the top of each puzzle and apply all of the instructions in turn, from top to bottom. Keep going until you reach the empty box at the bottom, then write your answer there. To make it extra tricky, try to do all of the sums in your head without writing anything down until each final answer.

In the first puzzle, for example, start with 14, then divide by 2 (to make 7), then add 15 (to make 22) and so on.

14	6	20
÷2	×2	+14
+15	÷3	-2
÷2	+4	+1
+19	×¼	-15
×2	×9	×2

TIME

FIND THE NUMBER

Sanj is thinking of a number between 1 and 30.

- It's in the **3** times table
- It's not in the **5** or **8** times tables
- It's an even number
- It's a two-digit number
- It's nearer to **30** than to 1

What is the number?

....

Hint: Start by writing out all the numbers in the **3** times table, then cross out the ones that don't fit the clues.

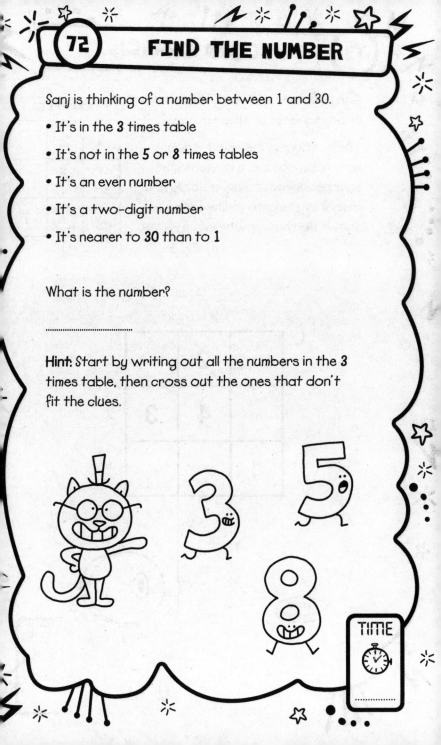

Can you find the coins hidden in the empty squares of these puzzles?

The numbers in the grid tell you how many coins are hidden in the squares horizontally, vertically and diagonally next to it. The example shows you how it works.

EXAMPLE:

1	2	◯
◯	4	
◯	◯	1

I.

	2	
	4	3
1		

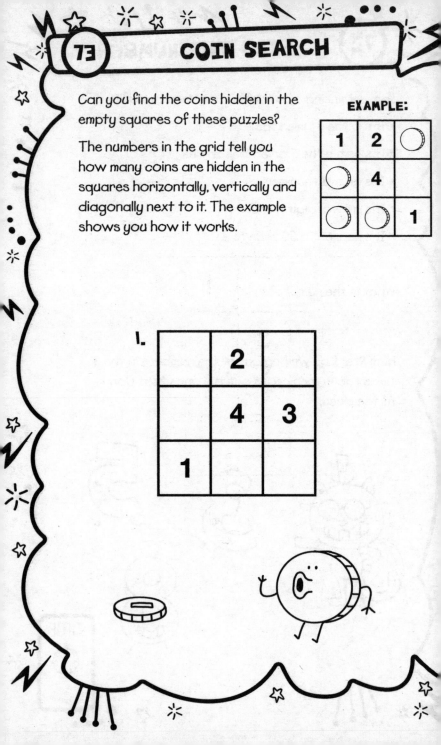

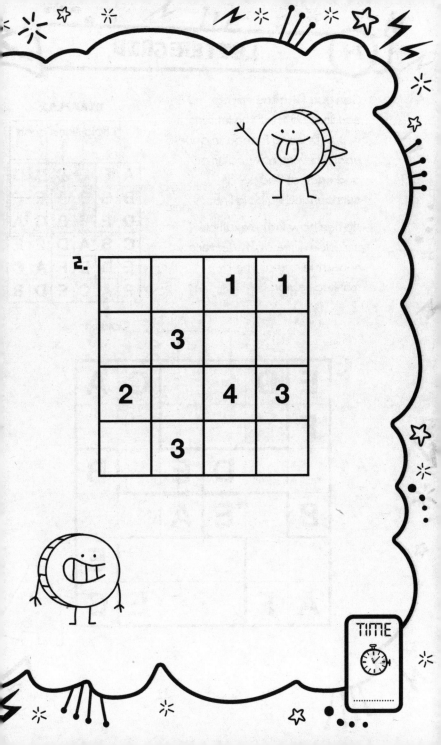

2.

		1	1
	3		
2		4	3
	3		

TIME

LETTER GRID

Can you fill in the empty squares so that the letters A, B, C, D, E and F appear once each in every row, column and each of the areas surrounded by bold lines?

Notice how in the example solution none of the letters repeat in any of the marked regions.

EXAMPLE:

Bold-lined area

A	F	E	C	B	D
B	C	D	A	E	F
D	E	F	B	C	A
C	B	A	D	F	E
E	D	B	F	A	C
F	A	C	E	D	B

Row

Column

I.

E	D			C	A
F					
		D	E		B
B		E	A		
					E
A	F			E	C

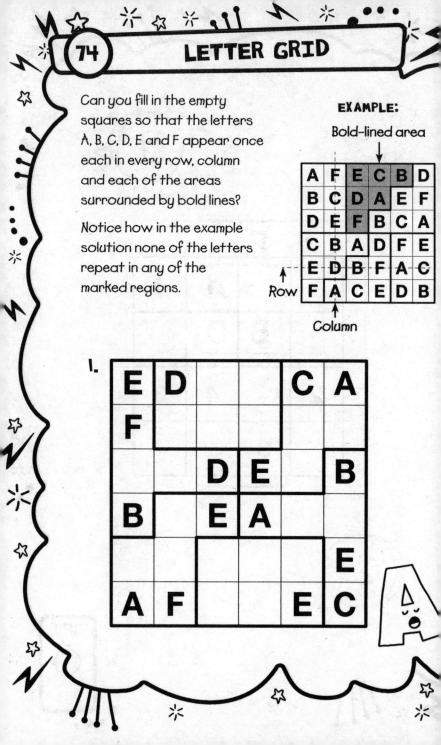

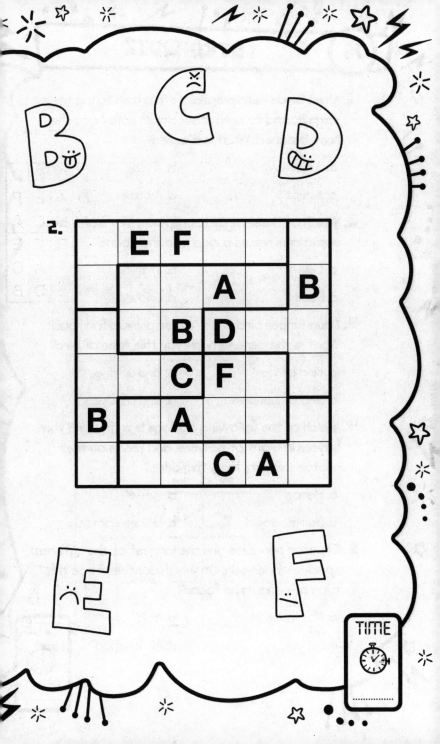

2.

	E	F			
			A		B
		B	D		
		C	F		
B		A			
			C	A	

BIRD QUIZ

1. Most birds build a special structure to lay their eggs in, and to keep their chicks safe once they have hatched. What is it called?

   a. A burrow   b. A hide

   c. A nest   d. A cabin

2. Which of these birds usually hunts at night, and sometimes makes a loud hooting sound?

   a. Owl   b. Starling

   c. Duck   d. Crow

3. Some larger birds hunt other animals for food. What is the general name for this type of bird?

   a. Bird of life   b. Bird of prey

   c. Bird of paradise   d. Bird of love

4. Which of the following options is a tiny bird that hovers in front of flowers, and feeds on their nectar using its long, thin beak?

   a. Heron   b. Hawk

   c. Hummingbird   d. House sparrow

5. Emperor penguins are the largest of the different species of penguin. On which continent can this type of penguin be found?

   a. North America   b. Asia

   c. Europe   d. Antarctica

TIME

....

Imagine merging these two pictures, so that the empty squares in picture A were replaced with the filled squares in picture B.

How many shaded triangles would you be able to count in the merged picture?

....

And how many circles would you be able to count?

....

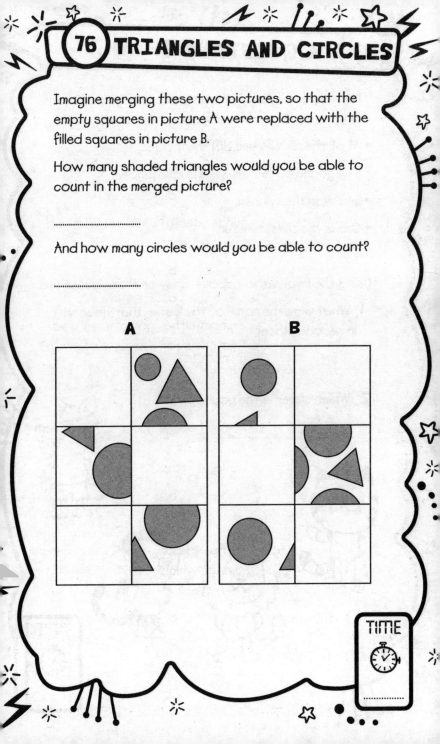

A

B

TIME

....

Three sisters – Amy, Bea and Caz – have just taken part in a race, in which only they took part.

- All of the sisters are different ages.
- The youngest sister came in last place.
- Bea was the winner.
- Caz is the oldest sister.

Using the information above, answer these questions:

I. What was the name of the sister that finished in second place?

....

2. Which sister is the youngest?

....

TIME

....

TOWER OF CUBES

You have 18 blocks built into a 3x2x3 tower, so they look like the example to the right.

You build three more identical block towers, then take some blocks away from each tower. How many blocks are left in each pile now?

EXAMPLE:

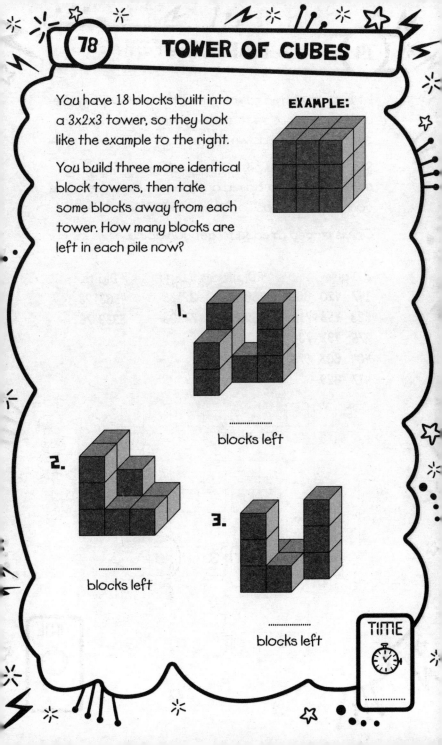

1.

.... blocks left

2.

.... blocks left

3.

.... blocks left

TIME

MAKE IT FIT

Fit all of the listed numbers into the grid, writing one digit per square so that every number can be read either across or down the grid.

Start by working out where each of the 7-digit numbers must go, based on what other numbers can connect to it. Cross off each number as you place it.

One is placed already to get you going.

3 Digits:			4 Digits:	5 Digits:	7 Digits:
147	420	661	3668	32185	4568123
338	458	715	8628	~~73308~~	8383876
375	491	736	9174		
404	608	978	9741		
417	629				

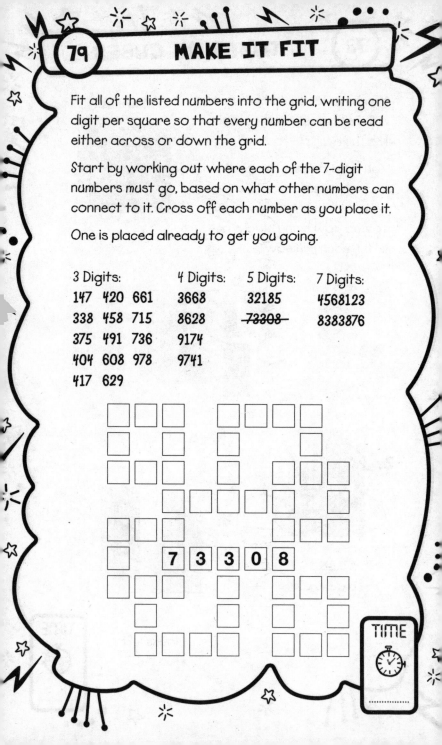

TIME

FIND THE CHANGES

Can you spot all ten differences between these two pictures?

TIME

SHAPE SPIN

What would pictures A, B and C each look like if rotated 90 degrees anticlockwise as shown by the arrow?

Which of the options, 1, 2 or 3, shows each rotated picture?

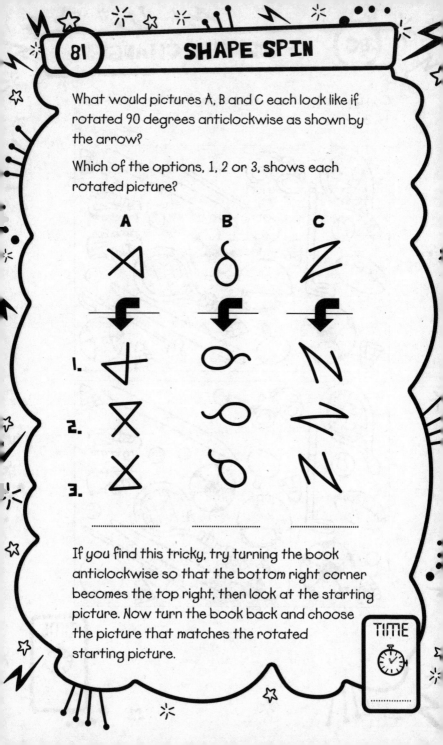

If you find this tricky, try turning the book anticlockwise so that the bottom right corner becomes the top right, then look at the starting picture. Now turn the book back and choose the picture that matches the rotated starting picture.

TIME

You have gone for a walk with a friend.

You only have one bottle of water between you, and you have agreed to share it so that you each have exactly half of the water. You filled it right to the brim before you left.

It's a symmetrical bottle with a screw cap, a narrow neck and a wide base, and even though it is also transparent it's hard to tell at a glance when it is exactly half-full.

There are no markings on the bottle, but there is a simple way to work out when it is exactly half full.

What is it?

TIME

How quickly can you find your way through this maze, entering at the top and exiting at the bottom?

Start

Finish

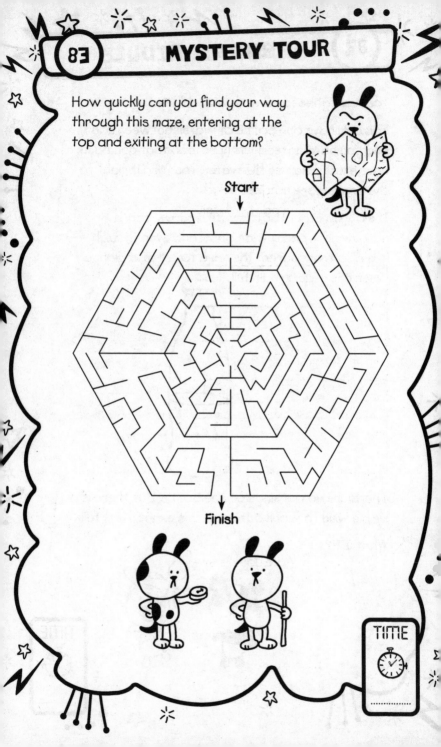

SHAPE SKILLS

It's time to test your shape-counting skills again.

Take a look at this picture. How many rectangles of all different sizes can you count in the picture? There are lots of overlapping rectangles, including the large one all around the outside.

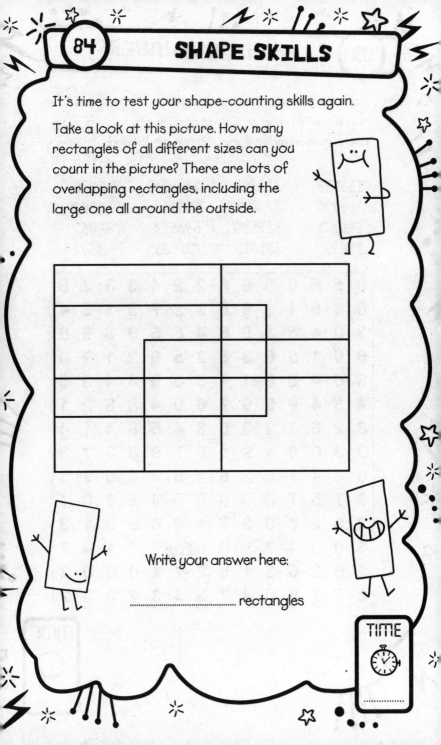

Write your answer here:

.... rectangles

TIME

FINDING NUMBERS

Can you find all of the listed numbers in the grid? They can be written in any direction, including diagonally, and can read either forwards or backwards.

153073	318395	384338	733422
184993	327833	564144	755063
260873	332540	598544	765652
296927	381016	701403	948577

9	5	5	6	9	9	6	2	2	4	3	3	7	8
0	4	6	1	1	9	8	3	2	7	8	3	3	4
3	0	4	5	3	9	8	4	5	5	9	5	9	0
5	0	1	5	6	3	5	3	5	9	2	1	9	0
8	6	4	8	8	1	1	5	3	9	3	4	3	6
4	3	4	9	5	9	7	8	0	4	8	8	2	1
3	2	6	3	2	3	5	3	4	5	8	4	1	4
3	3	0	0	1	9	1	6	7	9	3	3	7	3
5	3	4	7	5	2	6	7	5	3	9	6	7	3
9	7	5	7	3	5	8	9	8	4	5	3	0	1
3	8	2	7	0	3	7	1	2	6	9	3	1	3
3	0	3	1	7	5	0	5	5	7	9	1	4	7
2	6	3	6	3	1	5	2	7	1	0	0	0	3
3	2	7	9	6	4	7	3	1	3	2	3	3	2

TIME

ALL
THE
ANSWERS

ANSWERS

BRAIN TEASER 1

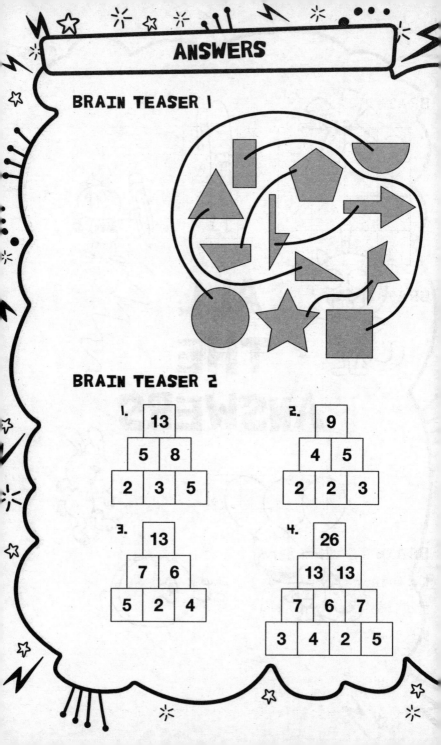

BRAIN TEASER 2

1.

	13	
5		8
2	3	5

2.

	9	
4		5
2	2	3

3.

	13	
7		6
5	2	4

4.

		26		
	13		13	
	7	6	7	
3	4	2	5	

BRAIN TEASER 3

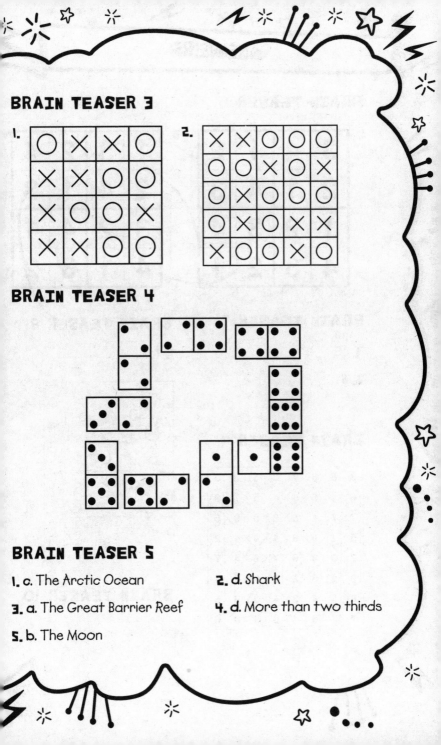

BRAIN TEASER 4

BRAIN TEASER 5

1. c. The Arctic Ocean

2. d. Shark

3. a. The Great Barrier Reef

4. d. More than two thirds

5. b. The Moon

ANSWERS

BRAIN TEASER 6

1.

3	4	1	2
2	1	4	3
1	2	3	4
4	3	2	1

2.

1	3	2	4
2	4	1	3
3	2	4	1
4	1	3	2

BRAIN TEASER 7

1. 10

2. 8

BRAIN TEASER 8

D, E, F

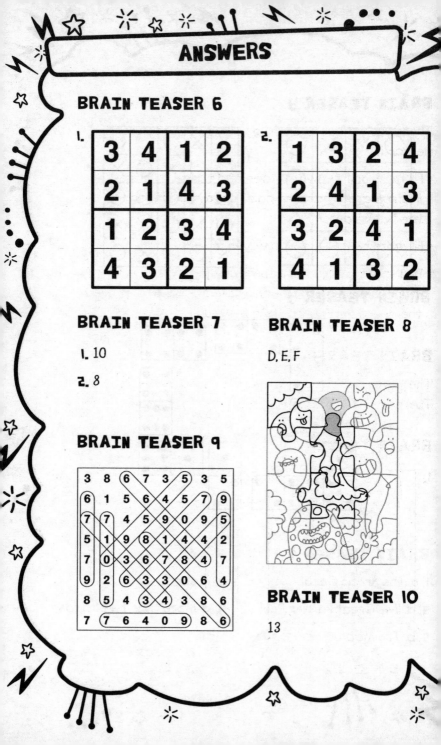

BRAIN TEASER 9

3	8	6	7	3	5	3	5
6	1	5	6	4	5	7	9
7	7	4	5	9	0	9	5
5	1	9	8	1	4	4	2
7	0	3	6	7	8	4	7
9	2	6	3	5	0	6	4
8	5	4	3	4	3	8	6
7	7	6	4	0	9	8	6

BRAIN TEASER 10

13

BRAIN TEASER 11

There are various ways to do this, but the quickest method is:

- Fill the 3-unit jug with water, and pour it into the 4-unit jug (so that now has 3 units in, and space for 1 unit more).

- Fill up the 3-unit jug with water from the tap again.

- Pour the 3-unit jug into the 4-unit jug until the 4-unit jug is full. This will only take 1 unit, and will then leave exactly 2 units in the 3-unit jug. Done!

BRAIN TEASER 12

The picture can be drawn using just four rectangles. There are nine different rectangles in the picture.

BRAIN TEASER 13

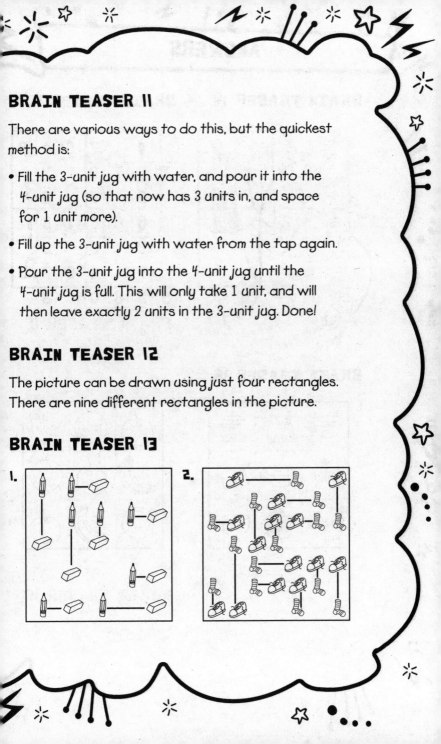

1.

2.

ANSWERS

BRAIN TEASER 14

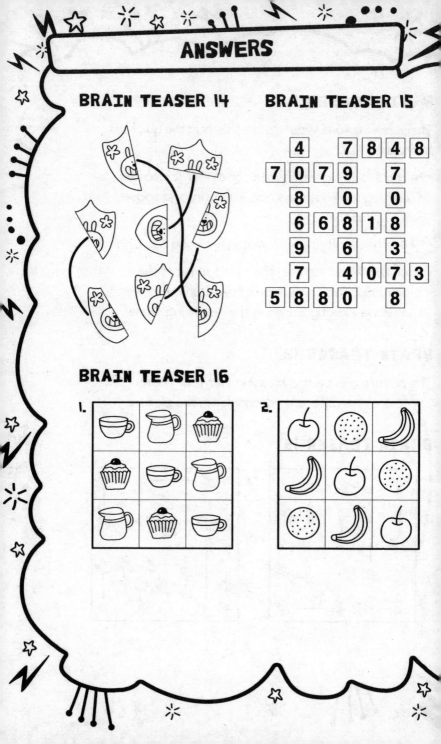

BRAIN TEASER 15

4		7	8	4	8
7	0	7	9		7
8		0		0	
6	6	8	1	8	
9		6		3	
7		4	0	7	3
5	8	8	0		8

BRAIN TEASER 16

1.

2.

BRAIN TEASER 17

- Zab. We know from clues 1 and 3 that Zob and Zib are at the back and middle of the queue, so Zab must be at the front of the queue.

- Green. We know that it isn't red, because Zib is in the middle of the queue and we know from clue 2 that the red light is at the front. Similarly, we know from clue 1 that the blue light is on Zob. So it must be the green light.

BRAIN TEASER 18

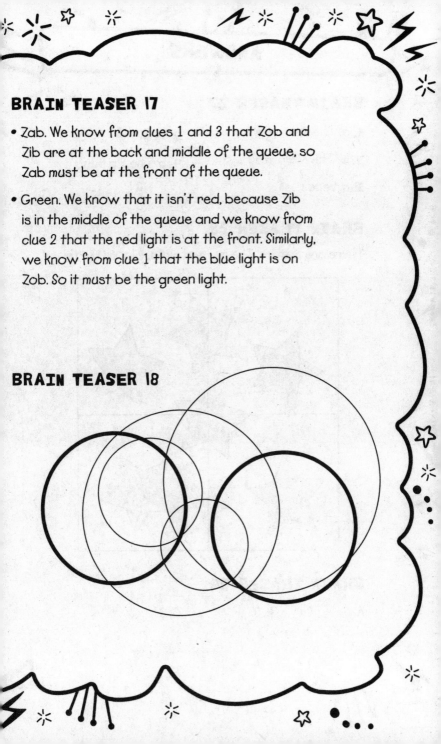

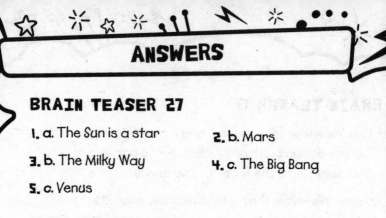

ANSWERS

BRAIN TEASER 27

1. a. The Sun is a star
2. b. Mars
3. b. The Milky Way
4. c. The Big Bang
5. c. Venus

BRAIN TEASER 28

There are 6 stars. The merged picture looks like this:

BRAIN TEASER 29

A. 2
B. 3
C. 3

BRAIN TEASER 30

19	13	5
33	23	30
21	46	6
7	39	3
3	78	21
6	66	7

BRAIN TEASER 31

The secret is not to move the cups around, but simply to pour the water between cups:

- Pick up the 2nd cup in the row and pour all of its water into the 5th cup

- Pick up the 4th cup in the row and pour all of its water into the 7th cup

Done!

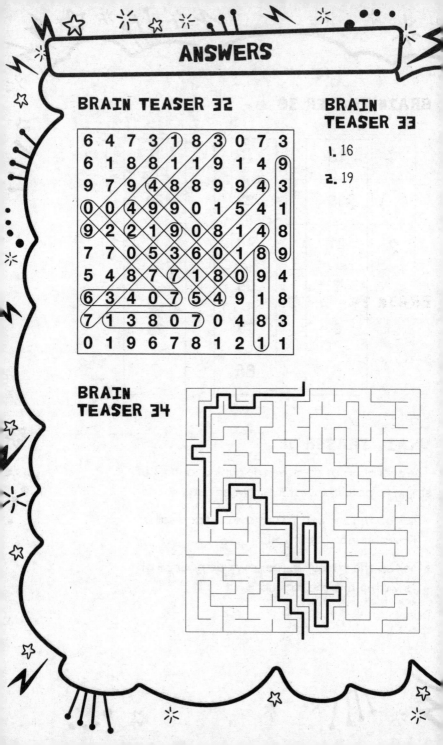

ANSWERS

BRAIN TEASER 32

6	4	7	3	1	8	3	0	7	3
6	1	8	8	1	1	9	1	4	9
9	7	9	4	8	8	9	9	4	3
0	0	4	9	9	0	1	5	4	1
9	2	2	1	9	0	8	1	4	8
7	7	0	5	3	6	0	1	8	9
5	4	8	7	7	1	8	0	9	4
6	3	4	0	7	5	4	9	1	8
7	1	3	8	0	7	0	4	8	3
0	1	9	6	7	8	1	2	1	1

BRAIN TEASER 33

1. 16

2. 19

BRAIN TEASER 34

BRAIN TEASER 35

1.

1		
◯	3	◯
2	◯	2

2.

1	◯	◯	2
2		3	◯
◯	2		2
2	◯	2	◯

BRAIN TEASER 36

1. b. France
2. a. North America
3. c. The Amazon
4. b. They are all volcanoes
5. a. The equator

BRAIN TEASER 37

4	4	2	3	9		
5		6		3	5	6
2	8	3	0	7		1
7		0		2		6
4		8	5	0	4	4
2	3	8		5		5
	8	1	1	0	2	

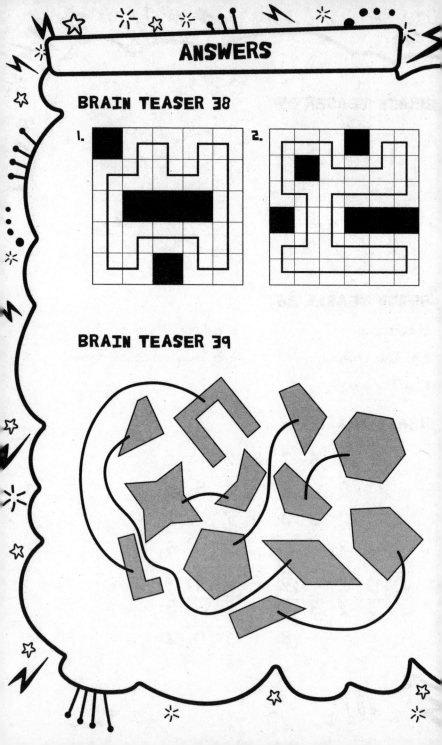

ANSWERS

BRAIN TEASER 38

1.

2.

BRAIN TEASER 39

BRAIN TEASER 40

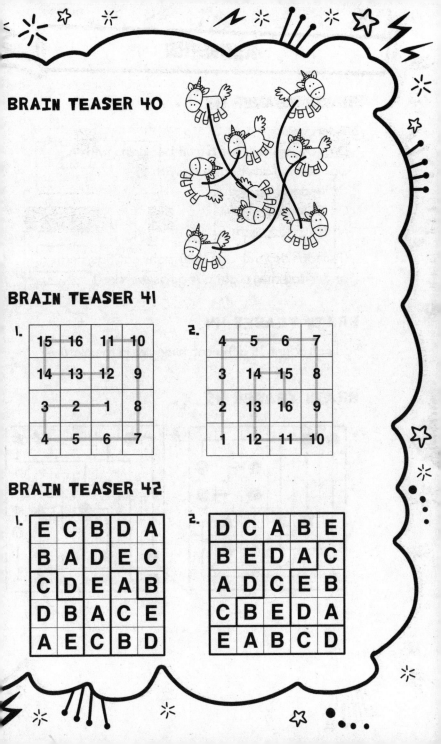

BRAIN TEASER 41

1.

15	16	11	10
14	13	12	9
3	2	1	8
4	5	6	7

2.

4	5	6	7
3	14	15	8
2	13	16	9
1	12	11	10

BRAIN TEASER 42

1.

E	C	B	D	A
B	A	D	E	C
C	D	E	A	B
D	B	A	C	E
A	E	C	B	D

2.

D	C	A	B	E
B	E	D	A	C
A	D	C	E	B
C	B	E	D	A
E	A	B	C	D

ANSWERS

BRAIN TEASER 43

c. Elderberries.

On Monday they eat a fruit beginning with 'A',
On Tuesday one beginning with 'B',
On Wednesday with 'C',
On Thursday with 'D',
And on Friday with 'E'.

(Perhaps on Saturday they might eat figs, and on Sunday they might eat gooseberries!).

BRAIN TEASER 44

You can count 15 different triangles in the picture.

BRAIN TEASER 45

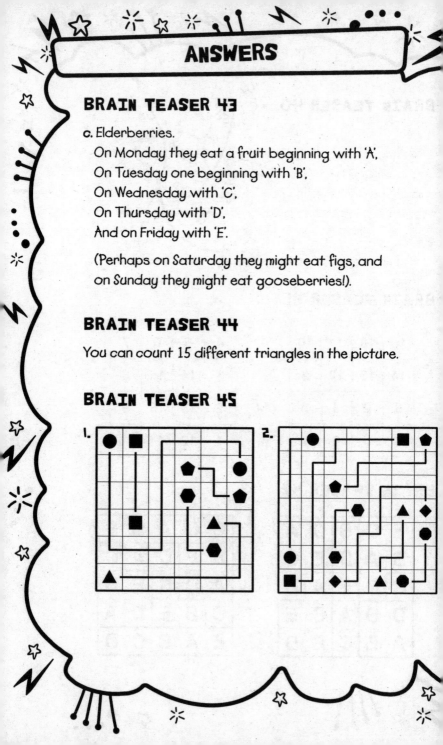

BRAIN TEASER 46

1. Red.

We know it isn't purple, since clue 2 tells us that Bbb is wearing the purple helmet. We also know that Ccc isn't the one wearing red (clue 3), so this means by elimination that Aaa must be the robot wearing red.

2. Bbb.

We know it isn't Aaa because its skill is to see the future (clue 1). It also isn't the robot with the orange helmet because they can become invisible (clue 4). We know that Bbb is wearing the purple helmet, not orange (clue 2), so by process of elimination it must be Bbb that can fly.

BRAIN TEASER 47

1. Balloons 3 + 18

2. Balloons 3 + 8 + 18

3. Balloons 3 + 18 + 20

4. Balloons 3 + 7 + 18 + 20

BRAIN TEASER 48

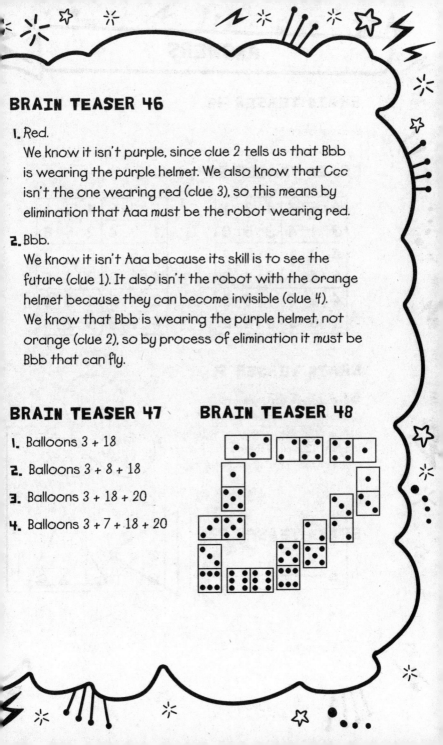

BRAIN TEASER 49

2

BRAIN TEASER 50

1.

2	5	6	4	3	1
3	1	4	2	5	6
6	3	1	5	2	4
5	4	2	6	1	3
4	2	3	1	6	5
1	6	5	3	4	2

2.

5	2	6	4	3	1
1	3	4	2	5	6
3	5	1	6	4	2
4	6	2	3	1	5
2	4	5	1	6	3
6	1	3	5	2	4

BRAIN TEASER 51

The secret here is to think in three dimensions. Start by placing three of the coins in a triangular shape, so they are all touching. Then, place the fourth coin in the centre on top of the others. Done!

BRAIN TEASER 52

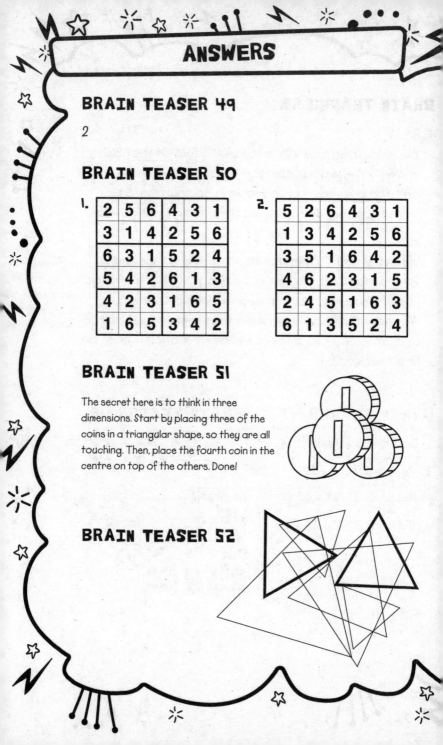

BRAIN TEASER 53

1.

```
      34
    16  18
   8   8  10
```

2.

```
      31
    17  14
   9   8   6
```

3.

```
        48
      25  23
    14  11  12
   8   6   5   7
```

4.

```
        25
      12  13
     5   7   6
   2   3   4   2
```

ANSWERS

BRAIN TEASER 54

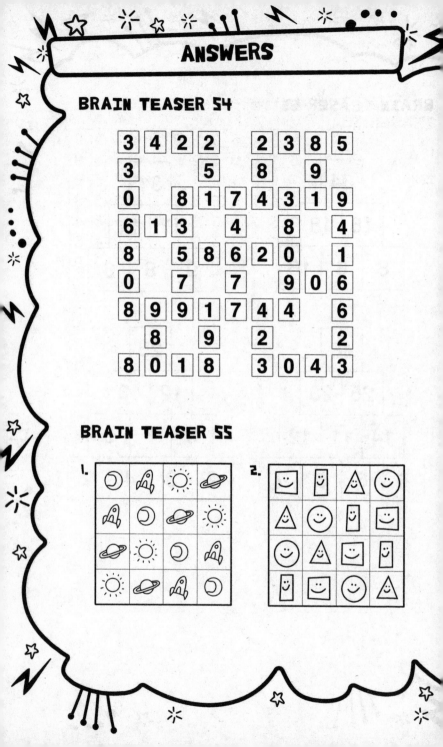

BRAIN TEASER 55

BRAIN TEASER 56

1. 15

2. 20

BRAIN TEASER 57

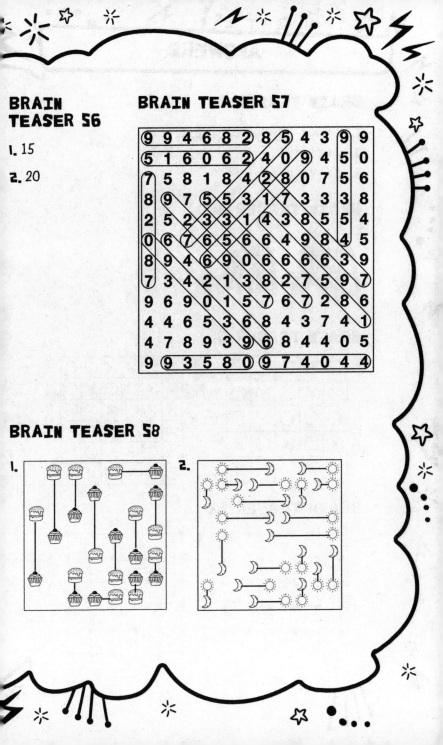

BRAIN TEASER 58

1.

2.

ANSWERS

BRAIN TEASER 59

1. c. Root vegetables
2. a. Grain
3. c. Onion
4. c. Italy
5. d. Orange

BRAIN TEASER 60

f.

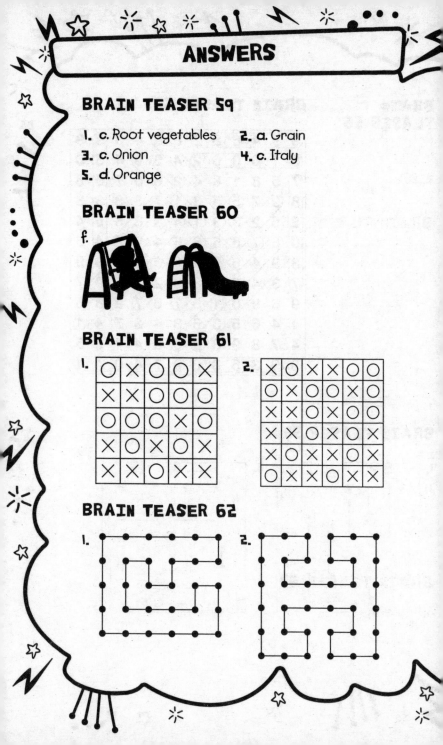

BRAIN TEASER 61

1.

O	X	O	O	X
X	X	O	O	O
O	O	O	X	O
X	O	X	O	X
X	X	O	X	X

2.

X	O	X	X	O	O
O	X	O	O	X	O
X	X	O	X	O	O
X	X	O	X	O	X
X	O	X	X	O	X
O	X	X	O	X	X

BRAIN TEASER 62

1.

2.

BRAIN TEASER 63

A. 1   B. 3   C. 3

BRAIN TEASER 64

1. $24 = 8 + 16$
2. $30 = 17 + 13$
3. $35 = 19 + 16$

BRAIN TEASER 65

1.

4	3	2	1
5	10	11	12
6	9	16	13
7	8	15	14

2.

3	2	25	22	21
4	1	24	23	20
5	6	7	18	19
10	9	8	17	16
11	12	13	14	15

BRAIN TEASER 66

The most you can place is 6 'X's.

After that you'll definitely have at least one line.

Here's one possibility:

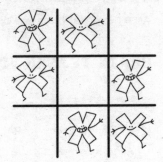

BRAIN TEASER 67

1. Balloons $9 + 11$
2. Balloons $6 + 7 + 9$
3. Balloons $8 + 10 + 11$
4. Balloons $8 + 9 + 10 + 11$

ANSWERS

BRAIN TEASER 68

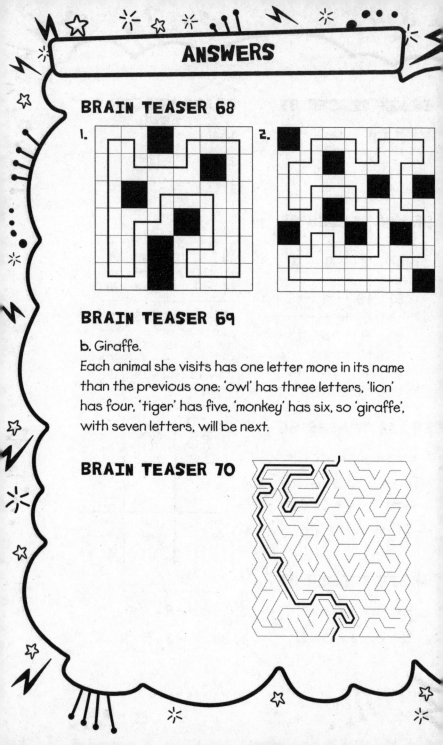

1. 2.

BRAIN TEASER 69

b. Giraffe.

Each animal she visits has one letter more in its name than the previous one: 'owl' has three letters, 'lion' has four, 'tiger' has five, 'monkey' has six, so 'giraffe', with seven letters, will be next.

BRAIN TEASER 70

BRAIN TEASER 71

14	6	20
7	12	34
22	4	32
11	8	33
30	2	18
60	18	36

BRAIN TEASER 72

18

BRAIN TEASER 73

1.

○	2	○
	4	3
1	○	○

2.

○		1	1
	3	○	
2	○	4	3
○	3	○	○

ANSWERS

BRAIN TEASER 74

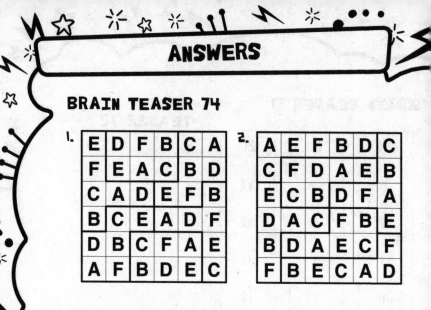

1.

E	D	F	B	C	A
F	E	A	C	B	D
C	A	D	E	F	B
B	C	E	A	D	F
D	B	C	F	A	E
A	F	B	D	E	C

2.

A	E	F	B	D	C
C	F	D	A	E	B
E	C	B	D	F	A
D	A	C	F	B	E
B	D	A	E	C	F
F	B	E	C	A	D

BRAIN TEASER 75

1. c. A nest

2. a. Owl

3. b. Bird of prey

4. c. Hummingbird

5. d. Antarctica

BRAIN TEASER 76

There are 4 triangles and 6 circles. The merged picture looks like this:

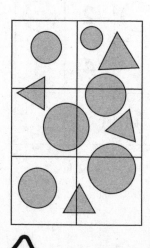

BRAIN TEASER 77

A. Caz.

We know Bea finished in first place from clue 3, so it must have been either Amy or Caz. We also know that Caz is oldest (clue 4), so from clue 2 we know that she wasn't in last place. By process of elimination Caz must have finished in second place.

B. Amy.

We know that Caz is the oldest (clue 4), and we know from clue 2 that the youngest sister came last but that this wasn't Bea (from clue 3).

So by process of elimination it must be Amy.

BRAIN TEASER 78

1. 9 blocks

2. 11 blocks

3. 9 blocks

BRAIN TEASER 79

6	0	8		9	1	7	4
2		3		7			2
9	7	8		4		4	0	4
		3	2	1	8	5		9
4	5	8				6	6	1
1		7	3	3	0	8		
7	3	6		6		1	4	7
	3			6		2		1
	8	6	2	8		3	7	5

ANSWERS

BRAIN TEASER 80

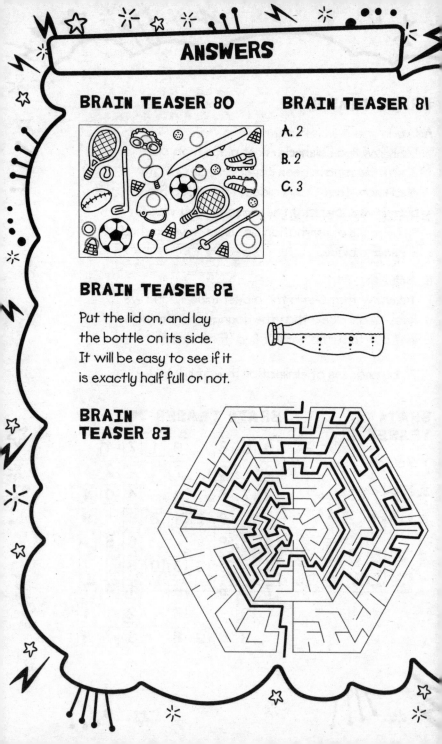

BRAIN TEASER 81

A. 2

B. 2

C. 3

BRAIN TEASER 82

Put the lid on, and lay
the bottle on its side.
It will be easy to see if it
is exactly half full or not.

BRAIN TEASER 83

BRAIN TEASER 84

You can count 44 different rectangles in the picture.

BRAIN TEASER 85

```
9 5 5 6 9 9 6 2 2 4 3 3 7 8
0 4 6 1 1 9 8 3 2 7 8 3 3 4
3 0 4 5 3 9 8 4 5 5 9 5 9 0
5 0 1 5 6 3 5 3 5 9 2 1 9 0
8 6 4 8 8 1 1 5 3 9 3 4 3 6
4 3 4 9 5 9 7 8 0 4 8 8 2 1
3 2 6 3 2 3 5 3 4 5 8 4 1 4
3 3 0 0 1 9 1 6 7 9 3 3 7 3
5 3 4 7 5 2 6 7 5 3 9 6 7 3
9 7 5 7 3 5 8 9 8 4 5 3 0 1
3 8 2 7 0 3 7 1 2 6 9 3 1 3
3 0 3 1 7 5 0 5 5 7 9 1 4 7
2 6 3 6 3 1 5 2 7 1 0 0 0 3
3 2 7 9 6 4 7 3 1 3 2 3 3 2
```

NOTES AND SCRIBBLES

NOTES

NOTES

NOTES

NOTES

NOTES

NOTES

NOTES

NOTES

NOTES

NOTES

NOTES

NOTES